NEURAL SUITCASE

THE KEEPER OF THOUGHT AND TIME

Purnendu Ghosh

NOTION PRESS

India. Singapore. Malaysia.

CONTENTS

WE ARE A BIOENGINEERING MARVEL

We are unique.

We have an upright posture and a protuberant nose.

We use language. We smile.

Laughter is our own. We gossip, blush, and shed tears.

We have opposable thumbs and use them to create tools.

We indulge in sex—not just for procreation, but for pleasure.

We can read other people's minds.

We aspire to surpass even ourselves, knowing full well it's not possible.

Some of these supposedly 'unique' human traits—culture, mind-reading, tool use, morality, emotion, personality—are also found in other animals. But the sophistication with which humans develop culture or tools is unmatched.

Take mind-reading: certain great apes and monkeys have demonstrated rudimentary signs—like the ability to deceive—suggesting some form of perspective-taking.

Animals do use tools: they crack nuts, dig holes, and even fish for termites. But their tools are not comparable to the ones humans create.

Animals also show personality. Many are not as characterless as we often presume. Social mammals, for example, understand rudimentary rights and wrongs in interactions: norms of food-sharing, defending territories, grooming, and caregiving exist.

Do animals have emotions? Yes—perhaps even plants do. But are those emotions tied to conscious feeling? That remains uncertain.

Many species outnumber humans. They dominate the Earth numerically. They mutate faster, reproduce more prolifically. Some may even follow rudimentary rules of conflict. But can they truly be considered our competitors?

We are a bioengineering marvel.

The last word of biology, the first word of sociology.

We are governed by the same biochemical reactions as other animals, but we are not the same.

Our difference is qualitative.

Our brain—and more importantly, our mind—makes us different.

Some argue that we're no better than animals, because we often behave worse. True—but sharing base instincts doesn't make us cats.

Michael Gazzaniga notes: the question is not whether we're fundamentally different, but how fundamental the differences are.

Our difference lies not in stronger muscles or tougher bones, but in the "phase shift" our brains have undergone.

Water is water—whether solid, liquid, or gas. Yet ice, water, and steam are worlds apart in form and function.

This is evolution's "phase shift"—a transformation so vast that it's hard to believe the before and after contain the same substance.

In complex environments, even similar substances behave differently.

Unless there's an incentive to become complex, complexity does not evolve.

Humans were once the weakest animals.

But we wanted to rule the Earth, and that desire became the evolutionary incentive.

There is nothing wrong with being at the top, if we know how to use both reason and instinct.

Man is a sum of inherited and acquired qualities.

He learns to integrate and to disintegrate.

His relationship with the world around him defines what he is.

Had man not walked the Earth, the Earth would have been a different place.

Nature once frightened man with its vastness. Now, it frightens man with its fragility.

We are different. Our ideologies differ. And often, they clash. This clash leads to animosity and acrimony.

Jonathan Haidt asks: Can't we all disagree more constructively? Getting along seems difficult, because of our morality. Morality both binds and blinds. It binds us to our group; blinds us to others. We think our group's ideology is best. We reject alternatives. This leads to what Haidt calls "groupish righteousness."

Our moral foundations become configured differently. We "agree to disagree," but rarely with empathy. Compatibility between temperamentally different people becomes difficult. What we need is a balanced mind.

A mind where empathy and systemisation coexist. Such a mind is disciplined, creative, ethical, and respectful. It can mirror the self and also act as a window to others.

Mindset can change outcomes.

Ellen Langer conducted an experiment in a nursing home. One group was encouraged to make decisions and care for houseplants. Another group was told the staff would care for everything.

A year-and-a-half later, the first group was more cheerful, active, and alert. Why?

Langer says: because of choice and the control it offers.

Making choices leads to mindfulness. Our physical health, she claims, can shift by changing our minds. She calls it the Psychology of Possibility.

In another experiment, elderly men lived for a week in a monastery that mimicked their youth—same decor, no modern conveniences. One group was told to act as if they were 20 years younger; the other simply reminisced.

The first group showed more significant cognitive and physical improvement. Why? Because acting as if they were young sent messages to the body.

Langer's research suggests: It is not our physical condition, but our mindset that limits us. Our ideas, fixed since childhood, affect how we age.

Context matters. "I can spot a candy bar from a great distance when I'm hungry," she writes. Her advice: keep your mind open to possibility.

Mindfulness is the active process of noticing new things, letting go of fixed patterns, and acting upon new insights.

Mindlessness, by contrast, blinds us to new options. It can damage our health and our lives.

Mindful health isn't about the right diet or medicine, but about breaking free from limiting beliefs.

Biology is not destiny.

MIND, THE KEEPER OF THOUGHT AND TIME

The mind, our neural suitcase, is mysterious and layered. It holds within it passing thoughts and quiet observations. It shelters life's questions, contradictions, and fragments of wonder. In its silent depths, understanding shimmers, memories breathe, and wars won.

The best idea sessions are held inside our neural suitcase. Our mind asks many interesting questions, works best in the shower, builds castles in the air, determines the size of our world, rebels against stagnation, and stretches with any new experience.

Our spiritual and religious traditions advise us to 'watch the thought, feel the emotion, and observe the reaction.'

Researchers studied people's ongoing thoughts, feelings, and actions. They asked simple questions like - what are you doing right now? Are you thinking about something other than what you're currently doing?

Their purpose was to understand the cognitive and neural bases of mind wandering. The studies tell us that we spend much of our time in the non-present. We spend much of our waking hours thinking about something other than what is happening in front of us.

Another group of researchers think that a wandering mind can protect us from immediate perils and keep us on course toward long-term goals.

Psychologists tell us that daydreaming is not enough. "Letting your mind drift off is the easy part. The hard part is maintaining enough awareness so that even when you start to daydream, you can interrupt yourself and notice a creative thought."

It is understandable that during 'flow' (a feeling of spontaneous joy, while performing a task) one's subjective experience of time is altered. Being happy makes one more creative. But it is not easy to control a wandering mind. At any given moment, so much information about the external world enters our brain. How can we stop ourselves from entertaining them?

Going to the Himalayas is one way of experiencing solitude, but it is too bothersome. Keeping a quiet mind amidst a storm is not easy. Moreover, such solitude may not serve the desired purpose.

Often, we are engaged in useless and futile conversations with ourselves. We often want to send our minds on a brief vacation. Minds that are on a short vacation, often yield very useful results. We may send our mind on a short vacation, but don't let anyone eat our head.

'Don't eat my head' is a commonly used expression. Interestingly, 'eating the head' has its source in a real instance found in nature. Sea squirts, these little animals, belong to the same group as humans. The sea squirt larvae resemble tadpole larvae. It doesn't evolve into a fish or amphibian. Instead, this little animal swims to find a good place to rest. Once it finds a good, solid surface, it attaches itself there. It wants to take a long rest, and thus remains there permanently.

This distant cousin of ours said to itself, what will I do with my head if I don't have to move? This smart thought made our cousin believe that there is nothing wrong if one eats their head. It did so and started eating its head. As a result of eating its head, it didn't grow; it remained larva.

We have learned an important lesson from our distant cousin. If we let someone eat our head, it means we have given the person enough indication that our head has become useless, and one can eat it. So, don't let anyone eat it. And never forget that your mind is one of your most important assets. If you lose it, you are lost. You can't move unless your brain allows it to. And as Ralph Waldo Emerson understood, little minds have little worries, big minds have no time for worries.

Our brain

The three basic units of the brain are the forebrain, the midbrain, and the hindbrain.

The hindbrain includes the upper part of the spinal cord, the brain stem, and a wrinkled ball of tissue called the cerebellum. The hindbrain controls the body's vital functions, such as respiration and heart rate.

The uppermost part of the brainstem is the midbrain, which controls some reflex actions and is part of the circuit involved in the control of eye movements and other voluntary movements.

The forebrain is the largest and most developed part of the human brain. It consists primarily of the cerebral cortex and the structures hidden beneath it. The cerebral cortex holds our memories, allows us to plan, and enables us to imagine and think. It is the source of intellectual activities.

The cerebral cortex is divided into two halves. The two halves communicate with each other through nerve fibres. These two halves are functionally quite different from each other. For example, the left half possesses the ability to form words, while the right half controls many of our abstract reasoning skills. The right half of the cerebral hemisphere primarily controls the left side of the body, and the left side primarily controls the right side. It means that when one side of the brain is damaged, the opposite side of the body is affected; a stroke in the right side of the brain can leave the left arm and leg paralysed.

Each cerebral hemisphere can be divided into sections, or lobes, each of which specializes in different functions. The two frontal lobes, which lie directly behind the forehead, do much of the work when we plan a schedule, imagine the future, or use reasoned arguments. In the rearmost portion of each frontal lobe is a motor area, which helps control voluntary movement. A nearby place on the left frontal lobe allows thoughts to be transformed into words.

The two sections behind the frontal lobes, the parietal lobes, are at work to enjoy the taste, aroma, and texture of the food. The forward parts of these lobes, just behind the motor areas, are the primary sensory areas that receive information about temperature, taste, touch, and movement from the rest of the body.

The occipital lobes, the two areas at the back of the brain, are at work when we look at the words and pictures. These lobes process images from the eyes and link that information with images stored in memory. Damage to the occipital lobes can cause blindness.

Our sense of music is through the activities of the temporal lobes that lie in front of the visual areas and nest under the parietal and frontal lobes. At the top of each temporal lobe is an area responsible for receiving information from the ears. The underside of each temporal lobe plays a crucial role in forming and retrieving memories, including those associated with music. Other parts of this lobe seem to integrate memories and sensations of taste, sound, sight, and touch.

Most of the actual information processing in the brain takes place in the cerebral cortex, commonly known as the 'Gray matter.' The structures that lie between the spinal cord and the cerebral hemisphere determine our emotional state and also modify our perceptions and responses depending on that state, and allow us to initiate movements that we make without thinking about them.

A pearl-sized part of our brain, the hypothalamus, does many important things like waking us up in the morning and controlling our adrenaline flow during an exam or an interview. The thalamus, which lies near the hypothalamus, is a major information track that goes to and from the spinal cord and the cerebrum. The basal ganglia are clusters of nerve cells surrounding the thalamus. They are responsible for initiating and integrating movements.

The amygdala, an almond-shaped structure in the brain, is an indicator of our social networking capability. Located deep within the temporal lobe of the brain, the amygdala is involved in the processing of emotions such as fear, anger, and pleasure. The amygdala is also responsible for determining what memories are stored and where they are stored in the brain. Studies have shown that damage to the amygdala impairs social functioning. The job of the amygdala is to signal to the rest of the brain when something that we are faced with is uncertain.

How the amygdala contributes to social networks is a mystery. It is not clear if a big amygdala is a cause or a consequence of having a large social network. It is not clear if certain people are born with larger amygdala and therefore create bigger social networks, or does the amygdala grow as one gain more friends and foes.

Neurons

Neurons are the primary functional units of the brain. All sensations, movements, thoughts, memories, and feelings are the result of signals that pass through the neurons.

Neurons consist of three parts. The cell body contains the nucleus, where most of the molecules that the neuron needs to survive and function are manufactured. Dendrites extend out from the cell body like the branches of a tree and receive messages from other nerve cells. Signals then pass from the dendrites through the cell body and may travel away from the cell body down an axon to another neuron, a muscle cell, or cells in some other organ.

The neuron is usually surrounded by many support cells. Some types of cells wrap around the axon to form an insulating sheath. This sheath can include a fatty molecule called myelin, which provides insulation for the axon and helps nerve signals travel faster and farther.

Axons may be very short, such as those that carry signals from one cell in the cortex to another cell less than a hair's width away. Or axons may be very long, such as those that carry messages from the brain down the spinal cord.

The Synapses

A synapse is the junction between two neurons where communications occur. When the signal reaches the end of the axon, it stimulates the release of tiny sacs. These sacs release chemicals known as neurotransmitters into the synapse. The neurotransmitters cross the synapse and attach to receptors on the neighbouring cell. These receptors can change the properties of the receiving cell. If the receiving cell is also a neuron, the signal can continue the transmission to the next cell.

Acetylcholine, a key neurotransmitter, makes cells more excitable; it causes glands to secrete hormones. GABA (gamma-aminobutyric acid), a neurotransmitter, tends to make cells less excitable. Serotonin is a neurotransmitter that controls sleep and temperature regulation. Dopamine is an inhibitory neurotransmitter involved in mood and the control of complex movements.

Synapses are central to brain function. Substantial synaptic rearrangement and pruning occur during development and beyond. Experience shapes the wiring of the brain: synapses are added and lost continuously. The peak of synaptic formation occurs between six and eight months after birth. Initial synapse formation happens independently of external input, but unused synapses are later eliminated.

Conversely, frequently used connections become stronger, with more dendritic spines and reinforced pathways. The principle is simple: "Use it or lose it."

This capacity for change is genetically regulated. Yet experience profoundly influences how these genetic potentials are expressed. With new gene-profiling tools, we can now study how neurons manifest and change. Understanding how genes and environment interact may transform how we diagnose and treat neurological conditions.

The wiring diagram

We draw the wiring diagram of the brain to understand how the brain functions. The wiring diagram of the human brain also sheds light on disorders that are presumed to originate from faulty wiring.

The wiring diagram of the brain is not easy to draw. The human brain is an intricate network of 100 billion neurons and 100 million synapses. Despite the difficulties envisaged, scientists are hopeful of completing the human brain's wiring diagram. The technological advances in neuroscience is one of the reasons for their optimism.

Understanding the working brain

The classical approach to understanding the neurological system focuses on identifying and mapping the connectivity of neurons involved in defined behaviours. By exciting individual neurons, scientists aim to determine their influence on behaviour. However, identifying specific neurons and perturbing them in the human brain remains difficult. Recording neuronal activity with sufficient spatial and temporal resolution poses a major challenge.

To address these limitations, multi-channel microelectrode recording arrays have been developed, allowing scientists to monitor the activity of multiple neurons simultaneously with high precision.

Imaging the living mind

Brain imaging techniques reveal how specific mental tasks selectively activate distinct regions of the brain. By observing these patterns, researchers can begin to "read" the subject's mind — distinguishing, for example, whether one is thinking about a face or a place.

Key imaging technologies include:

Electroencephalography (EEG): Measures electrical activity via scalp electrodes.

Computerised Axial Tomography (CAT): Uses X-ray imaging with computer assistance.

Positron Emission Tomography (PET): Traces radioactive markers injected into the bloodstream.

Magnetic Resonance Imaging (MRI): Uses magnetic fields and radio waves to map brain structures.

The integration of structure and function is achieved through Functional MRI (fMRI). This non-invasive technique provides high-resolution data on neural activity by measuring changes in blood oxygenation, a proxy for the metabolic demands of active neurons.

fMRI not only aids in the diagnosis of neurological disorders but also enables assessment of the brain's responses to stimuli. This is crucial for drug development and has expanded cognitive neuroscience into areas such as motivation, reasoning, and social behaviour. fMRI can even reveal hidden thoughts, truths, lies, and desires.

A Brain in Flux

The human brain is far from complete at birth. Much of its growth occurs during the first three years of life, reflecting dynamic adaptation to the environment. The average newborn brain weighs under 400 grams, while an adult brain reaches around 1400 grams. After the age of twenty, brain weight gradually declines.

Earlier, it was believed that we are born with a fixed number of neurons, hardwired for life, and that with age, neurons and connections are simply lost. This view has changed.

Contemporary neuroscience shows that the brain is highly plastic. It can form, eliminate, and strengthen connections throughout life. Neurons modify their connectivity, morphology, and synaptic strength in response to experience, not just during early development but across the lifespan.

Freedom, responsibility, and the brain

Neuroscientist David Eagleman observes, "Perhaps not everyone is equally 'free' to make socially appropriate choices."

Genes don't tell the whole story. The environment completes the narrative. Our experiences can even

change gene expression, altering the very foundation of
who we are.

No part of the brain functions in isolation. Consider a
struggling child: Is the problem a lack of motivation, or
a neurobiological learning disability? These questions
may find clearer answers as neuroimaging becomes
more refined and reliable.

Knowing without knowing

It is not always necessary to know the destination
before beginning a journey. Every effect may have a
cause, but understanding that cause isn't always
required. As Mackenzie noted over two centuries ago,
one may not know how to make a machine, yet still
succeed in making one. In other words, it is possible to
solve new problems independently of previously
acquired knowledge.

Alan Turing offered another deep insight. He believed
there is a relationship between formal concepts and
intuition — that we need not understand the machine's
inner workings to appreciate its function. For Turing,
machines are abstract computational devices, useful for
probing the limits of what can be computed.

Turing saw a path — from absolute ignorance to
artificial intelligence — suggesting that understanding
might emerge not just through knowledge, but also
through exploration.

Though incomplete at birth, the brain carries within it the seeds of infinite transformation. Its structure adapts, its functions evolve, and its pathways are shaped by both inheritance and interaction. As our tools grow more precise, so does our understanding—not just of the brain but of what it means to be human.

Software and Hardware

The hardware of the invisible mind is the biological framework — the brain and its intricate neural networks. Comprising billions of neurons connected through synapses, this structure is shaped by evolution and moulded further by our environment. It is the seat of perception, sensation, memory, and movement. Like hardware, it has limits — in capacity, speed, and durability — yet within these limits, it performs astonishing tasks with stunning efficiency.

But unlike a machine, this hardware evolves. It prunes itself in childhood, rewires in adulthood, and adapts in moments of crisis. Trauma can burn its circuits; learning can reinforce them. It dreams, imagines, and sometimes misfires. It is tangible and measurable, yet even under the most powerful scans, its full story remains elusive.

The software runs thoughts, emotions, beliefs, memories, and the instructions that guide behaviour. This software is written in languages — spoken, emotional, and symbolic. It is shaped by our upbringing, education, stories, relationships, and the cultures we inhabit.

It carries contradictions, hidden biases, and emotional bugs. It continues to function nevertheless. We inherit parts of it without consent. And occasionally, we experience a version update — a revelation, a reorientation, often triggered by grief, love, or learning.

The interface: invisible, yet expressive

An invisible mind communicates through visible expressions — speech, art, posture, hesitation. What lies beneath is always partially hidden. Two minds connect through filters, projections, and assumptions. Misunderstandings arise because they are uniquely configured.

Like machines, minds can stall. They can be overclocked by anxiety or slowed by depression. They can suffer from memory corruption, emotional lag, or loss of purpose. The good thing is that they can be healed, through conversation, collaboration, or shared silence.

New ideas are born. Empathy expands. Innovation occurs. This synchrony does not require perfection; it requires resonance.

Packing the mind

The mind is one of our most important possessions. Despite its immense power, the brain's neuronal capacity has remained largely unchanged over thousands of years. What has evolved is the way we use it—through language, culture, tools, and shared knowledge. Yet, much of its potential remains unrealized. While we have expanded its reach with technology, we still underuse its depth—in creativity, empathy, critical thinking, and self-awareness. The true frontier lies not in what more the mind can do, but in how we choose to use it.

Using the brain near its potential does not mean relentless mental exertion. Like a muscle, the mind grows stronger with thoughtful use and intentional rest. Overuse without recovery can drain willpower and cloud judgment, but balanced engagement—combining challenge with reflection—enhances clarity and resilience. Wisdom lies not in overdrive, but in knowing when to think, when to feel, and when to simply be.

 Potential is one thing, its utilisation another. Having the capacity to think, imagine, and reflect is not the same as doing so meaningfully. While we have expanded the mind's reach with technology, we still underuse its depth. The true frontier lies not in what more the mind can do, but in how wisely we choose to use it.

Is thinking an exclusive property?

It is not. You can think what a big man can think. The difference lies not in what you think, but in how you stay with the thought, and what you do after it arrives.

Thinking is a cumulative phenomenon. What we call our thinking is never ours alone. It is shaped by a larger, invisible whole. Its depth depends on a mysterious entity called the mind. Though invisible, the mind draws its structure from something visible, the brain.

So don't ever believe that you can't think. You can think, like any storyteller. You can choose your thoughts. You can reject the ones that don't serve you.

Your capacity for thought isn't limited by the size of your brainome. In fact, your brainome is as vast as the sky. Use it—don't let it rust from neglect. And if it does gather rust, don't worry. There are ways to de-rust it.

So, pack this incredible instrument—your mind— wisely. It has unlimited absorption capacity. But that doesn't mean you must fill it with clutter. A little junk may be fine—perhaps even necessary, to keep the instrument flexible and real.

Caring for this most vital possession is your responsibility. The size and quality of your world depend entirely on the capability of this inner instrument. So go ahead—write the edited version of what you think.

Imagining an ideal mind

Think of Sadi Carnot, who envisioned the ideal engine—not to build it, but to understand the boundaries of what could be.

Likewise, the ideal mind doesn't chase perfection for possession, but for perspective. It seeks purity not in outcomes, but in possibilities.

At times, our mind echoes authentic thoughts: better to
be naturally stupid than artificially intelligent; better to
be a fool with a soul than a machine with a mind.
Organic imperfection can surpass manufactured
competence. The very notion of the ideal depends on
the presence of the non-ideal.

Even for an ideal fluid to flow, it needs a touch of
friction to be real. Carnot imagined the perfect engine
to define the limits of thermodynamic potential.
Similarly, the ideal mind dares to imagine perfection,
only to understand how insight is born in the tension
between the imagined and the real.

In one of my wanderings, I assigned myself a task: to
assemble an ideal neural network. I selected neurons
with care. Ironically, when given a free hand, the task
became harder. The more perfect the parts, the more
elusive the whole.

Man, once seen as a freak of nature, is now considered
the pinnacle of evolution. Yet the paradox remains:
evolution has made him both the most complex and, in
many ways, the simplest of beings.

Man seeks to preserve his uniqueness, yet longs to
belong. He evolves to understand, to influence, perhaps
even to dominate

A LIVING NETWORK

We are a mix of many minds

Though we make a number of decisions every day, we are not as rational decision-makers as we wish to be. Our decisions are coloured.

What goes on in our minds when we take decisions? What specific neuronal circuits in our brains are responsible for our thoughts and actions? Decision neuroscience investigates the neural basis of human decision-making.

The part of the brain that is linked to emotion is the nucleus accumbens (nacc), the peanut-sized area that becomes active when we expect a reward of a primary nature. The part of the brain that is linked to anxiety, the anterior insula, lights up when a person sees disgusting, repulsive stimuli or when someone anticipates physical pain.

Pure rational decision-making is difficult, as decisions are always coloured with emotions of the person who is taking the decision. People with damaged part of the brain responsible for emotional reactions are unable to decide; the rational mind vacillates endlessly over the possible rational reasons. Extremely emotional decisions, on the other hand, lead us to wrong decisions.

Both 'cold reasons' and 'hot emotions' are needed to make the 'right decision'.

We do mental simulations for many different actions before we actually make a choice. Some parts in our brain, being 'perceptual system specialists', place a value on what we see. We tend to assign a value to different options we observe. Rewards are often the major parameter that affects our decisions. We thus develop a tendency to manipulate our decisions in the hope of better rewards. Our decisions depend upon how we value our choices.

A decision involves many processes. One needs to accumulate evidence for or against different choice options, evaluate their possible outcomes and risks and suppress certain learned responses and biases. Thus, it is important to understand how different parts of the brain do different computations in a coordinated way.

There can't be a set of universal laws of decision-making. Brain is like a toolbox with random tools. You take out one particular tool to solve a specific problem. The problem is, how so many tools interact to solve an interrelated problem. Our brains are not big enough, and we don't have requisite neurons to represent every situation that we might possibly encounter.

We need to understand why different individuals make different decisions, and why they make different choices when they face the same situation. Are the differences due to genetic differences, or due to the differences in experiences and learning environments, or both?

It gives a good feeling that trustworthy decisions emanate from a trustworthy mind.

Trust begets trust. Trusting the self is the first requirement of trusting others. You can't trust others unless you trust yourself.

Matters related to trust occupy a huge amount of our mental energies. DeSteno makes a very important observation: "Although it's true that cooperation and vulnerability require two parties, no one ever said that the two parties had to be different people. To the contrary, the parties can be the same person at different times."

One of the big challenges our ancestors faced was the need to solve the dilemmas of trust. Because of this dilemma, the mind constantly tries to ascertain the trustworthiness of others. Trust has inherent risks. But trust is also kind of a risk that is worth taking.

In the matters of trust, illusions are as good as hard facts. There are trusts that are 'calculation-based'. These trusts calculate the value of creating and sustaining trust in a relationship relative to the costs of sustaining or severing the relationship.

The 'identification-based trust', on the other hand, values another person's identity as an individual. More trustworthy and sustainable relationships grow out of identification-based trust.

Then there is 'benevolence-based trust'. In this, an individual does not intentionally harm another when allowed to do so.

The other kind of trust is 'competence-based'. In this, an individual believes that another person is knowledgeable about a given subject area and therefore, can be trusted.

Under vulnerable circumstances, we tend to depend more on trust. We shift from one mode of trust to the other, depending upon our life circumstances.

Competence and reliability are the two traits that determine and establish trustworthiness. Both competence and trust are important for managing a system. One of the most essential ingredients of a knowledge-based system is knowledge sharing. Knowledge sharing is not possible unless trust is embedded in the system.

Trust evokes a feeling of confidence. A trusted person enjoys many advantages; even his vulnerability is accepted. A person can be trusted in some contexts, but not necessarily in all the contexts.

Distrust, on the other hand, evokes a feeling of doubt and fear. The reasons of distrust could be purely imaginary, resulting out of misplaced feelings. Such feelings unnecessarily create vulnerability.

A little distrust is often helpful. It can avert herd mentality. Relationship experts say that a healthy amount of distrust can protect against the risk of exploitation.

Does trust need periodic validity checks?

Yes, it does if the trust is event-based, as the continuance of event-based trusts generally depends on future events. If the trust is process-based, it is more likely to become permanent.

Bias is one of the main reasons for our taking wrong decisions.

Our biases and prejudices are subjective. Because of distorted perceptions and wishful thinking, we see things more positively than they are. We even distort our memory to suit our perception. We accept the arguments of those whom we like and reject the arguments of those whom we dislike. We attribute our success to our abilities and talents, and our failures to bad luck, external factors and destiny. We use one yardstick to judge the success/ failures of the self, and another yardstick for others. We underestimate the influence of self-interest on our own judgments and decisions, but overestimate its influence on others. We underestimate future uncertainties. We cross-check the bad news, but readily accept the good news.

We all have blind spots. We take biased decisions based upon the irrational decisions we have taken in the past. We accept things, not necessarily based on merit, but merely because of our familiarity with the thing. We take hasty decisions to escape the feeling of doubt and uncertainty. We overestimate the degree to which others should agree with us. We underestimate others' ability to understand us. We overestimate our own ability to know others. What was said matters less than who said it.

Almost all our decision-making biases favour conflict rather than concession. Hawks see only hostility in their adversaries. Doves often point to subtle openings for dialogue. A bias in favour of hawkish beliefs and preferences is built into the fabric of the human mind, says Daniel Kahneman.

Biases don't die. They take new forms. We find it almost impossible to ignore the subjective first people's views of things.

Decision is a subjective perception and experience. Some of us like familiarity and certainty. Some of us like uncertainty and novelty. People in the first group are less receptive to new ideas and are biased towards predictability and clarity. People belonging to the second group love to face new situations and are biased towards such people/issues.

A mind is not a machine. It is a beautiful network.

A BALANCED MIND

Fritjof Capra once wrote about two great friends who held profoundly different worldviews. "Heisenberg gave me a vivid description of discussions between Erwin Schrödinger and Niels Bohr," he recalled. Schrödinger's wave mechanics relied on a continuous and familiar mathematical formalism, while Bohr, building on Heisenberg's matrix mechanics, embraced a discontinuous framework based on the idea of quantum jumps—strange, abrupt, and unorthodox.

In a humorous and touching scene, Bohr tried relentlessly to persuade Schrödinger of his interpretation. Heisenberg smiled as he described it: "How poor Schrödinger was lying in bed at Bohr's home, and Mrs. Bohr was serving him a bowl of soup, while Niels Bohr sat beside him insisting, 'But Schrödinger, you must admit…'"

This story reminds us that conflicting ideas need not lead to animosity. People can disagree deeply and yet get along beautifully. Consider Rabindranath Tagore and Mahatma Gandhi. Both giants of their time held each other in the highest regard, yet diverged on many issues. After the Bihar earthquake, Gandhi attributed the disaster to divine displeasure over untouchability— "not a leaf moves but by His will." Tagore, disturbed by the same tragedy, respectfully disagreed. For him, the connection between natural calamities and ethical failure was untenable.

In some debates, there is never a final winner, only a deepening of thought.

Michael Madhusudan Dutt and Ishwar Chandra Vidyasagar present another telling example. Dutt, flamboyant and often adrift, led a turbulent life. Vidyasagar, though not conventionally modern, championed widow remarriage—a radical reform of the time. Despite their differences, Vidyasagar extended support to Dutt, helping him find clarity amid chaos.

Such stories show us that the convergence of contradictory ideas and the compatibility between differing temperaments is possible—if both individuals are well-meaning.

So, what kind of minds do we need for the present century?

Howard Gardner offers a framework that feels increasingly relevant. He identifies five essential types of minds for the modern world:

The Disciplined Mind: Not merely about accumulating knowledge, but mastering modes of thinking unique to each discipline—science, history, mathematics, the arts.

The Synthesising Mind: One that connects dots, weaving fragmented information into coherent wholes.

The Creative Mind: A mind that ventures beyond the known, asks new questions, and imagines novel solutions.

The Respectful Mind: One that seeks to understand and value differences, not just tolerate them.

The Ethical Mind: One that reflects on its responsibilities as a citizen and a professional, seeking the common good.

Yet these minds are not always in harmony. The disciplined mind may clash with the creative one; the synthesiser seeks closure, while the creator delights in uncertainty. The challenge is to cultivate all five in balance.

Ultimately, what we need is a balanced mind—one that can think rigorously and feel deeply, one that upholds both empathy and system. A mind that can engage across divides without diminishing difference. A mind that can not only solve problems, but also ask: For whom? At what cost?

A balanced mind gets along despite differences—and that may be the greatest need of all.

THE MIND OF TIME

The mind can move through time in any direction. Time can be compressed or stretched. Time slows down when there is not much work to do. Time races when there is enough challenging work. An emotional event becomes more recent than it is. Time flies when one is having fun. The perception of time can heighten enjoyment and ease annoyance.

Hudson Hoagland's wife had the flu. She made a usual complaint that her husband is away from her bedside for too long, even if he had gone away only for a short while.

A common complaint gave birth to such an important experiment.

Hoagland proposed to his wife quite an annoying experiment: Count off 60 seconds while he timed her with his watch. The result of the experiment: When her minute was up, his clock showed 37 seconds. In subsequent experiments he showed that his wife's mental clock ran faster, higher her temperature became.

Our illusions and distortions of time are consequences of the way our brain builds a representation of time. Time slows down during brief, dangerous events such as car accidents and robberies.

Our brain processes different types of sensory information at different speeds by different neural architectures. The difficulty our brain faces is that it receives signals from different modalities at different speeds in different neural regions, but to be useful, these signals must become aligned in time and correctly tagged to outside events.

We are time travellers. We can visit the future or revisit the past whenever we wish. We get trapped in the present when our neural time machines are damaged.

Aristotle argued that time neither has a beginning nor end. The end of one moment is the beginning of another moment. One doesn't want to retain all the past memories. One also doesn't want to completely wash off his past. One can't stop future vistas from taking shape.

Past and present are like a 'seed and tree' situation. All seeds have the potential to become trees, but not all seeds become trees. If the soil is not right, the seeds rot. For a seed to become a tree, proper soil and sunlight are needed.

Janus is the God of the beginning and the end. Janus (the month of January is named after him) is usually depicted as having two faces or heads, facing in opposite directions. It was the gift of God Saturn that Janus could see both the future and the past.

Janus symbolises change and transition, such as progression of the past to the present into the future. Janus can see various facets of time in the same frame and at the same time.

Time is a friend as well as an enemy. The trick is to harness it and to work in line with our conception of time.

As one gets older, time seems to speed up. One may call it 'forward telescoping'. The 'backward telescoping' is when you guess that events happened longer ago than they did.

 Some say it is the tempo of life that makes time faster or slower.

We can't, and possibly shouldn't, try to live long in the past or the future. The past and the present are known and thus limited. The future is unknown and thus unlimited. It is hard to fathom the 'unlimited' based on the 'limited'.

EYES HAVE SPECIAL MINDS

Eyes are a great social navigator. Eyes can read others' minds as well as allow others to read their mind. Eye-gaze perception is our guide to social interaction.

Eye contact signals attraction between people. Looking straight into the eyes indicates that you are a straight person. Prolonged eye contact, on the other hand, is perceived as aggressive and can be threatening. Disengaged eye contact is a sign of distraction. It happens when we try to conceal our true feelings.

Eyes tell us that we are being noticed. We prefer to look at objects, rather than empty space. When a person is seen to move their eyes to engage in eye contact, they are perceived as more likable and attractive than if they are seen to disengage eye contact.

Eye contact influences perception of another's attractiveness. This effect is modulated by the perceived relationship between the observer and the observed party. The capacity to use another person's eye gaze, as a cue to attention, develops early in life. Children can detect deception. They know from the eyes what people want to hide from them.

We possess a great sense of gaze direction. Our visual system is sensitive to gaze direction of other people. It is also known that other person's gaze shift produces a shift of an observer's usual attention in gaze direction.

Gaze cueing is a phenomenon whereby we pay attention to our peers by following their gaze and looking in the same direction as them. The work of scientists reveals that we pay more attention to people who have a higher status in life. The studies suggest that students pay more attention to faces when they are told that they are looking at high achievers. The researchers say, "We rapidly encode the relative social status of the individuals populating our environment, and we shape our social attention processes accordingly."

The meeting of eyes tells different things to different people. One can see in it curiosity, while the other may see in it challenge. Trust can be developed almost immediately through eye contact. To look into someone's eye is generally viewed impolite. If you hold eye contact too long (usually more than five to seven seconds), it may be interpreted as a stare and can become a source of discomfort to the person being eyed.

Often, a shy person or a person who lacks confidence is afraid to make eye contact.

Liars and people who have social anxiety problems, experience trouble maintaining eye contact.

In a classroom, one can tell from the student's eyes if the teacher has talked enough.

Then, there is eye contact favouritism; looking at certain people more than others. We tend to look more at those people who give us the most positive feedback, and also at people who matter the most. On the other hand, if you ignore some people (as demonstrated by the lack of eye contact) they too close the eyes on you.

'Eye contact equality' is a sure way to demonstrate fairness and respect to the listeners.

At many places (many of our villages) eye contact has different implication; it can even be taken as a sign of disrespect.

In the staring contest, blinking is taken as a sign of submission.

Benjamin Franklin said, "Keep your eyes wide open before marriage, and half shut afterwards."

Seeing is a gradual and an elaborate process. According to a Buddhist text, before a man finally sees he goes through several intermediate steps. A man comes, having come he listens, by listening he remembers, he examines the sense of things, he ponders, he mentally realises the highest truth and penetrating it by means of wisdom, he finally sees.

Some people can 'see' despite their visual disability. They have a weird ability to respond to visual information despite having no conscious knowledge of seeing anything.

Beatrice de Gelder, in a carefully conducted experiment, found that a visually impaired man could walk unaided through obstacles lying on the way. She says that the brain has a number of alternate routes that can be mobilised when the main avenues to vision are blocked. It is because the projection of images is not only restricted to the visual cortex, but also to other parts of the brain related to vision and emotion. She says that the mind could subconsciously process some visual information. Though we tend to concentrate on major visual systems in the brain, we have hidden resources.

Our conscious vision depends on a region of the brain, called the primary visual cortex. If this region is damaged, how can one see? How could people see without knowing that they can see? This feat is possible due to the auditory assistance.

Some blind people have the ability to sense the reflection of sound waves, and that assists them to locate obstacles. Experiments have also revealed that people can unconsciously detect a wide range of visual attributes, including colour, simple shapes, simple motion, and the orientation of lines or gratings. Large shapes, as well as very fine details, seem hard to detect.

Some people can't see, but don't want to believe that they can't see. They bump into objects while walking, but deny the visual impairment.

The visual disturbance is a result of brain abnormality or damage rather than eye abnormalities. They have a rare symptom of brain damage. Neuropsychiatrist Gabriel Anton and the brain pathologist Francois Babinski tried to understand this uncommon visual loss.

Anton's syndrome (AS) is caused by damage to the occipital lobe, which extends from the primary visual cortex into the visual association cortex. It is mostly seen following a stroke, but may also be seen after head injury. AS patients not only are unable to volunteer the information that they can't see, they also mislead others by behaving and talking as though they are not blind. They not only experience difficulty in finding their way around, they begin to describe people and objects around them, which as a matter of fact, are not there at all. AS patients lack self-perception of their deficits.

Some have the ability to perceive motion in the blind field, crudely but consciously. Another manifestation of impaired visual perception is Charles Bonnet Syndrome (CBS). CBS patients experience visual loss with complex hallucinations like images of unfamiliar people or buildings.

"Not the eye, only the mind, can determine the grade of significance."

Some people can see with a special eye; the mind's eye. These people are an inspiration even for people with eyesight.

The French author Jacques Lusseyran became blind when he was only seven. He could feel light "rising, spreading, resting on objects, giving them form, and then leaving them". He saw light only when he was happy and thought well of people. But the light faded when he was afraid, angry, and impatient. When he was jealous or unfriendly, it was as if "a bandage came down" over his eyes.

Lusseyran lost his sight, but in exchange got many other extraordinary abilities. He seemed to hear well. "My ears were hearing no better, but I was making better use of them". He believes that the blind suffers greatly "from the inexperience of those who still have their eyes."

Lusseyran's important message: Parents should never say, "You can't know that because you can't see" and "Don't do that, it is dangerous."

Lusseyran says, "For a blind child, there is a threat greater than all the wounds and bumps, the scratches and most of the blows and that is the danger of isolation."

Zoltan Torey became blind when he was 21 years. He met with an accident in a factory. One day he thought, "It was not quite fair for me to turn to God for assistance now that I was in a pretty deep mess, when, in fact, I had had no need for the relationship before."

He asked himself, "instead of asking what God and the Universe can do for me, why don't I ask what I can do for God and the Universe?"

Torey's doctors advised him to leave all visual imagery behind and rebuild his mental representation of reality using hearing and touch. The doctors' instructions did not appeal to Torey. He did just the opposite; he simply pictured the world around him through his now hyperactive visual imagination.

Torey discovered his world by continuously visualising the surroundings, "a world which became increasingly intense, accurate, and sharp." He took time to master this art. After some months, he was living in a virtual reality.

"Often, people forget that I can't see. I wear sunglasses all the time, and once somebody even said to me - it was very funny - she said, "Don't 'look' at me that way."

Torey believes that vision gets in the way of people with eyesight; "without being troubled by the continuous bombardment of actual sight, enables you to have a kind of mental freedom that can be very creative. Often, people close their eyes when they think. So, in that respect, I was able to utilise my abnormal situation as a real advantage."

Torey's most useful message is that "fate is one thing", but "what we make of it is another."

THE SENSIBLE MIND

We like to see, hear, taste, smell, and touch the world. Through these five basic senses, we read the story that goes around us. But mere observation is not enough; it only tells part of the story. If we want to understand the story more comprehensively, we need to soak our observations with emotional sensibilities. A sense without this understanding is like a machine that collects information but doesn't know how to use it.

Senses give us sense data. When memory joins sensation, it becomes experience. When the mind acts on experience, it becomes knowledge. When the mind acts on knowledge, it becomes thought.

To make sense of the senses, we require abilities of a different order, without them, we should be unable to recognise form, pattern, regularity, harmony, rhythm, and meaning, not to mention life, consciousness, and self-awareness.

That ability is our sixth sense, the conscience. It is the sense of 'mind-in action'. It is the sense of right and wrong. It is the policeman of the community of senses. Its voice is the 'voice within', which can lead different people in quite different directions.

Unless we have the seventh sense, the common sense, the other six senses are of no use. This sense, though called common, it is not always common. What is obvious to one person may not be so obvious to the other person. Since our perceptions differ, our sense of perception is also different.

'Uncommon sense' and 'Common nonsense' are the two outcomes of common sense.

Uncommon Sense is an 'out of the box' type. Someone has rightly observed - such people are so deeply in the box that they can never get out of it.

Common nonsense types are abundantly available. Such varieties are a "reflection of a flawed brain with a capacity for being interested in more things than it can comprehend."

What William Makepeace Thackeray had to say on this subject: "I never know whether to pity or congratulate a man on coming to his senses."

A FICTIONAL MIND

We love to dwell in fictional worlds and cherish having a fictional mind. Fiction is a selective transformation of reality.

Every thought arrives with an image. The moment we hear or read a story; our minds begin to visualise scenes and characters. This process often continues even after the story ends.

A writer creates a world where fiction and reality coexist. For a fictional world to feel credible, it must possess emotional complexity and elements of surprise. It is often said that a story should be sufficiently complex to engage attention, evoke suspense, and excite emotion—yet not so complex that it loses unity, clarity, or coherence. "The story must be probable, but it also must be a story. In other words, fiction is like history, but it is not history," writes Mortimer Adler.

Imagination plays a crucial role in the acquisition and expansion of empirical knowledge. It is the reader who bridges the gap between conception and execution.

Fictional experiences enhance our mental fitness. Like software loaded into a system, the more stories we absorb, the more neural connections we forge. Our brains function more efficiently with a richer network of such internal connections.

Spending time in fictional realms, then, is an investment. Evolutionary psychologists John Tooby and

Leda Cosmides observe that such investments yield greater returns earlier in life, when opportunities are fewer and cognitive adaptations are still forming. The more fictional narratives we encounter, the more situations we become familiar with, without needing to live through them.

What's remarkable is that our brain knows how to separate pretence from reality. It can store not just universal facts, but also information that may be true only in a specific context, moment, or to a particular person. This flexible handling of truth is what makes us so adaptable.

OUR EXTERNAL MIND

Proponents say the Internet helps us move ahead in life. Opponents caution that its impact depends on how much—and for what purpose—we use it.

The real worry is that we are becoming overwhelmingly dependent on the Internet. It is shifting our cognitive functions from searching for answers within the mind to searching outside it. Much like calculators reduced our reliance on mental arithmetic, the Internet diminishes our capacity for deep thought.

It has liberated us from the need to commute for information and literacy, but in doing so, it has fragmented our thinking process.

Many argue that information overload has begun to erode our capacity for reflection and introspection. Some believe it has dulled our risk appetite. Bombarded by real-time updates, where is the time to pause, to rethink, to innovate?

Should we allow human intelligence to be submerged by computational intelligence? We are flooded with ideas but lack the cognitive bandwidth to assimilate them all. We know that ideas and information generate stress, and managing this deluge demands immense self-discipline.

One way to cope is through "alone time"—periods of intentional disconnection, designed to reconnect with the self. It's in these moments that one begins to

prioritize, to ration information, to understand the
necessity of selective attention.

As one CEO warns, "You have to guard against the
danger of overeating at an interesting intellectual
buffet."

Infovores—the new breed of 'vores' in the digital
space—feast on information. But when they consume
more than they can digest, they suffer from infobesity.

Just as obesity stems from poor eating habits and lack
of activity, infobesity results from undisciplined intake
and passive engagement. It's not just what we consume
that matters, but how we consume it.

Nicholas Carr suggests that if we are turning into
informavores, it is likely because we want to. But even
infovores can learn to take smaller bites—savouring
information, not stuffing it.

Has the Internet changed the way we think?

Some say it has enhanced our cognitive fitness and
remains value-neutral. Others warn that "speed plus
mob" is a dangerous cocktail.

It delivers things faster, but not always the right things.
In a world obsessed with the "real-time," the now
eclipses the then. The past loses significance.

Many see in the Internet a fading connection with the natural world—an extinction of experience, of presence.

The Internet may have made us lazy, distracted, lonely, even unhinged—but it has also made us smarter, more connected, and more capable than ever before.

Ernst Pöppel captures this ambivalence beautifully:

"It is like swimming in an ocean with no visible horizon. Sometimes, suddenly, an island surfaces unexpectedly, indicating a direction. But before I reach it, the island disappears again. This feeling of being at a loss has become much stronger with the Internet."

Pöppel refuses to swim in an ocean without direction. He seeks islands—anchors, frameworks. He reminds us that in this world of too much, we must build our framework for orientation.

Only then can we swim without drowning.

A QUESTIONING MIND

All questions are personal. Often, we reveal more about ourselves in the questions we ask than in the answers we give. Why do we ask questions? Why are we not content with what we already know?

The ability to think inquisitively is one of our critical survival skills.

Some questions have no answers. Some have both "yes" and "no" as valid responses. Some are deeply satisfying, while others are deeply disturbing. Some questions reflect our reasoning, understanding, and learning. Others expose our hollowness.

We ask both convergent and divergent questions.

Convergent questions have specific answers.

Divergent questions are open-ended and invite multiple possibilities.

Closed questions are saturated—they end discussion. Open-ended ones are unsaturated—they open doors.

Sometimes, the questioner doesn't expect an answer—the answer is implicit. Sometimes, they expect only agreement. Such questioners are either too confident in their beliefs or too insecure to tolerate dissent. Either way, they avoid alternatives.

A questioning mind asks both small and large questions.

Understanding the Questioner

If we struggle to understand a question or a point of view, where does the problem lie—in asking or in understanding? What gives us more stress: knowing too much, or knowing too little?

Why do we eat junk food when we know it's bad for us?

What is more difficult—talking, or listening?

Why is it hard for a crab to walk straight?

Why is boredom an essential human experience?

Why is an evil genius more dangerous than a fool?

Why is providence the most popular scapegoat?

Why is the unexpected so exciting?

Why can't we be right all the time?

What hidden motive prompts our generous deeds?

Does speed increase or decrease efficiency?

Why is the person we hate most often ourselves?

Why does our mind ask the best questions when it has nothing to do?

Why do the truly beautiful often avoid makeup?

Some questions are clichéd. Some arise from genuine curiosity.

The Cliché Collection

Here are some tired old questions—and a few fresh responses:

Where do you see yourself after ten years?

I see you sitting in front of me, still asking clichéd questions.

What would happen if the Earth stopped spinning?

We would all start spinning instead.

What will happen if there is no sun?

We'll get to watch the noon show in an open-air theatre.

Have you ever handled a conflict?

This is all I've been doing since my marriage ten years ago.

Why couldn't they fire you?

Because I was always wet.

If honesty is the best policy, why is it not followed?

Because those in charge aren't honest enough to follow it.

The Parade of Platitudes

Some statements are so overused that they've lost all meaning:

My daughter-in-law is like my daughter.

Mother Teresa is my role model.

It's a sheer chance that I'm in this profession.

And the most overused of all:

It's not about winning or losing; it's the spirit of participation that counts.

The Interview Trap

In one of Satyajit Ray's films, the protagonist attends a job interview. One of the interviewers asks, "What is the weight of the moon?" The hero wonders: What does that have to do with the job?

Some interviewers want to test what the candidate
knows. Others want to show off their own knowledge.

I wasn't selected after my first interview. But I must
say—it was the best interview I ever faced. It prepared
me to handle future ones with confidence. The
questions raised hope in me.

Questions Without End

We all ask questions.

Engineers ask questions. Doctors ask questions.
Planners, teachers, students, editors—all ask questions.
So do law-abiders and law-breakers. Leaders and
followers.

We ask existential questions. We ask trivial ones. We
ask zero-hour questions. We ask questions to probe, to
provoke, to pretend.

This tradition will continue. And there will never be the
last question.

MIND OF A HAPPY FAMILY

A happy family is a dynamic structure. It breathes, bends, and reshapes itself continually under the influence of individual growth, life events, shifting relationships, and external pressures. Attempting to impose fixity on such a structure can result in stagnation or conflict, as it resists the natural ebb and flow of familial life. Fixity in a dynamic structure is, therefore, inherently paradoxical. In the context of family, happiness is not a fixed state but a fragile, ever-evolving balance—requiring continuous nurturing, adjustment, and resilience.

This paradox echoes in the workings of the human mind. The mind is in constant motion, seeking fixity—meanings, patterns, identities—to anchor itself. Yet, it flourishes only when it remains elastic. Similarly, the family offers emotional coherence and identity, but its inner health depends on adaptability. The mind mirrors the family: rooted, yet restless. The family mirrors the mind: cohesive, yet unpredictable.

Is this paradox the reason joint families are disintegrating and nuclear families emerging?

Yes. The shift from joint families to nuclear families reflects this tension between fixity and dynamism. Joint families, with their hierarchical structures and shared responsibilities, offered a collective way of living that provided stability—but often at the cost of individual autonomy. They required constant negotiation among members with differing values, interests, and personalities.

With the rise of urbanization, economic mobility, and changing social norms, individual autonomy has gained precedence. People now place a higher value on privacy, personal freedom, and the ability to shape their own lives. Nuclear families offer a more dynamic and flexible structure, enabling members to pursue individual goals without the burdens and compromises required by extended family living.

At the heart of this shift lies the desire for individuality—the defining force of our age. Today's society celebrates personal expression and self-determined paths, whether in career, lifestyle, or relationships. While joint families once offered emotional and logistical support, they can also inhibit this quest for selfhood. The nuclear family, for many, strikes a more manageable balance between belonging and freedom.

Yet, the embrace of individuality comes with trade-offs: reduced intergenerational wisdom, weaker familial safety nets, and the risk of social isolation. Fixity is still desired—but perhaps in smaller, self-made constellations. The mind, like the modern family, keeps reconfiguring itself in search of a structure that both anchors and frees.

Fixity, then, is not a destination but a longing. It lives not in permanence, but in the promise of return—in the idea that something, somewhere, even within flux, can still feel like home.

A TEACHER'S MIND

My experience has taught me that a teacher who knows their subject well but does not know their students is not a good teacher. Good teaching is not just about knowledge delivery — it is about awakening minds. It is about understanding how those minds are wired, how they feel, struggle, adapt, and grow. Teaching, at its best, is neuro-emotional engagement.

Neural anatomy reminds us that every learner is different. Learning speed, memory, attention, and emotional responses are shaped by the architecture of each individual brain. A teacher's mindset must align with this diversity — responsive, compassionate, and flexible. Students cannot learn unless the teacher captures their attention, and attention cannot be commanded — it must be invited.

Effective teachers recognize that some students need time to grasp even simple ideas. Mirror neurons — the brain's way of empathizing — help the teacher sense frustration, joy, or confusion. The act of teaching becomes a subtle reading of signals, a kind of quiet translation of the unspoken.

Climbing is difficult for those at the baseline. Maintaining position is a challenge for those at the top. But those in the middle of the ladder are the most vulnerable — they face uncertainty from both ends. They are neither settled nor certain. Teaching, therefore, is about supporting all — encouraging the hesitant, stabilizing the high achievers, and anchoring the drifting.

Should one follow in another's footsteps or chart their own course? This is a question every learner — and perhaps every teacher — must face. Drawing differs from tracing. When we draw, we encounter discontinuities. These gaps disappear when we trace, but some of us prefer to live with discontinuities — they become the very force that moves us forward on our own terms.

Conviction and confidence are not imposed; they arise from self-realization. But conviction alone is not enough. One needs a matching intellect — and teaching involves chiselling both. A mismatch between will and intellect leads to inner discontent. No one can be saved by another's beliefs. The intellect is not an extension of faith — it is a muscle to be trained.

My profession has taught me that not everything is for sale. Our internal reward systems — quiet neural loops of meaning and integrity — are powerful. They keep us from dishonesty, even when no one is watching. We must protect these inner circuits, so our positive self-image does not corrode.

It gives me deep satisfaction to be a teacher. I have learned that a teacher's commitment to their students, and a student's responsibility toward their teacher, go far beyond the classroom. The relationship is built on attention, trust, responsibility, and care. These are not only ethical choices — they are neurological needs.

The brain seeks meaning. The heart seeks connection. A teacher's mindset offers both.

WHEN KNOWLEDGE EXCEEDS THE MIND

Bertrand Russell once warned, "If knowledge continues to increase, the world will need wisdom in the future even more than it does now." His caution was not about the expansion of facts, but about the diminishing capacity to comprehend their meaning. As we navigate an era of exponential information growth, the distinction between knowledge and wisdom becomes not only relevant but vital.

Wisdom is not simply a possession of facts—it is the art of distilling meaning from them. It requires a confluence of cognition, self-reflection, and openness. The wise are not those who know the most, but those who can discern patterns, recognize perspectives, and choose what to overlook. If knowledge is an accumulation, wisdom is filtration.

The path to wisdom is subtle. One may acquire it by interacting with the wise, by living deeply, or by learning through trial. It is said that wisdom is more easily learned than taught—but when not taught, it is often learned the hard way. Knowledge can be printed and stored; wisdom must be embodied and lived.

A Jewish proverb captures this difference with elegance: The clever person can extricate himself from a situation into which the wise would never have entered. Cleverness is tactical; wisdom is strategic. Knowledge equips the mind; wisdom prepares the soul.

Wisdom does not come automatically with age, though the association is potentially positive. With age, the biological hardware of the brain may deteriorate, but the software of the mind—refined through reflection, empathy, and experience—can deepen. As one wisdom researcher puts it, "One can have theoretical knowledge without any corresponding transformation of one's personal being. But one cannot have wisdom without being wise." Wisdom, in other words, is not just in what is said, but in how it is said and lived.

Are we wiser than our ancestors? The present generation certainly knows more. It has access to information undreamed of in the past. But understanding is not just about access—it is about assimilation. We can cure previously incurable diseases, yet often forget how to lead a simple, contented life. The gain in knowledge has not always translated into a gain in wisdom.

Can knowledge ever exceed man?

To know something, one must have the capacity to know. Just as seeing requires an eye, knowing requires a cognitive organ. The fact that something is inaccessible to us does not imply it does not exist. What lies beyond the range of our cognition remains real— just unrealized.

Imagine a graph where the X-axis represents the size of the knower's head, and the Y-axis represents the knowledge of the world. At the origin lies a person with neither cognitive capacity nor knowledge. As the head size increases, so too does knowledge—ideally in proportion. But human variation complicates this neat model.

Some know what they know—consciously competent. They may have limited information but profound self-awareness. Others don't know what they know—unconsciously competent—gifted yet unaware of their potential. Then some know what they don't know—conscious of their ignorance—often the best learners. Finally, the most concerning group are those who don't know what they don't know—unconsciously incompetent—ignorant and unaware.

Some people choose a narrow world and know it deeply. They may care little for the wider universe but excel in their own niche—music, painting, philosophy. Their "head" may not be large, but it fits perfectly the world they inhabit.

As knowledge expands and as humans seek to keep pace, the need arises for an "external head"—repositories like libraries, machines, and now artificial intelligence—to manage this overflow. If the growth of knowledge outpaces the growth of our cognitive and reflective capacities, an imbalance sets in. We become custodians of knowledge without comprehension.

And perhaps the gravest irony emerges when a person is engaged for their head—and then their head is rendered inconsequential. In such moments, the tragedy is not merely of misuse, but of missed wisdom.

MIND AND NOSTALGIA

The mind is a restless collector. It is curious, alert, always moving forward. Memory, a curator of moments, storing fragments of experiences. Between the two, a silent negotiation unfolds.

Then nostalgia enters. A song, a fading photograph. And suddenly, memory becomes emotion. Nostalgia wraps the past in warmer hues, softens the sharp edges of reality, and restores what was lost.

Mind, memory, nostalgia - together, they shape our time. In the spaces between what was and what is, we find ourselves pausing, wondering, sometimes aching.

Nostalgia has its own kind of remedy.

Sometimes healing comes not from medicine, but from memory, movement, and a pinch of spice.

THE FRAGILE MIND

A friend recently asked me about the old building near our childhood home. Strangely, I couldn't recall it—a structure once so familiar, now vanished not only from sight but also from memory. Borrowing from Marcus Aurelius' Meditations, I replied, "How swiftly all things wash away, both the bodies themselves in the universe, and the remembrance of them in time."

Our mental apparatus has almost unlimited capacity for reception and retention. So how do memories fade? Memory failure is like breathing failure: unnoticed until it happens. I often wonder—what is harder, remembering or forgetting?

The Nature of Memory

Memory serves different purposes. The purpose decides which pathway the brain takes. We are, in many ways, the sum total of our fixed memories—ranging from the profound to the trivial.

Short-term memory mirrors current thinking and holds fleeting details. Long-term memory, shaped by years of experience, retains the gist more than the details. It often feels fuzzy, yet studies suggest otherwise: we have a massive storage capacity, and many long-term memories retain precision and detail.

We forget when we can't retrieve a memory. New memories can override old ones, especially when they involve similar content. Old memories sometimes obstruct new learning. Forgetting can also arise from 'encoding failure'—when information fails to enter memory in the first place.

We all know the frustration of not recalling a familiar name—a temporary blocking of stored information. Conscious attempts to forget often backfire, reinforcing the very memory we want to erase. We become prisoners of memory.

The Seven Sins of Memory

Daniel Schacter outlines the seven "sins" of memory—imperfections that arise from a system that usually works efficiently.

Transience: Memory fades with time. This decline is gradual. Over time, memories shift from specific to reconstructed, from fact to inference.

Absentmindedness: Often due to failure of prospective memory—we forget to remember. It explains why we lose track of small tasks.

Blocking: The tip-of-the-tongue feeling—where we know we know something, yet can't retrieve it. Often happens with names.

Misattribution: Attributing a memory to the wrong source. A major cause of eyewitness error.

Suggestibility: When misleading information distorts memory. A leading cause of implanted memories.

Bias: Memory is edited and rewritten, often unknowingly. Our current beliefs and emotions distort past experiences. A person disillusioned in a relationship may retrospectively paint the entire past negatively.

Persistence: Some memories, especially emotional ones, refuse to fade. They intrude repeatedly, often painfully.

These "sins" are not flaws but features—part of the way memory functions efficiently.

The Malleability of Memory

Memories are fragile at the moment of formation but strengthen over time through consolidation. Once consolidated, they remain static until recalled. But every recall is a reconstruction, not playback.

Emotional impact can be altered by recontextualizing a memory. Research suggests each retrieval changes the memory. Sometimes dramatically.

In fact, the only way a memory stays unchanged is by never being used. The most accurate memories may be the ones never recalled.

Neuroscientists studying reconsolidation observe that new information added during recall reshapes the memory. The result is a collage of old and new.

Our brains are not like tape recorders; they are more like editors with agendas. They distort during acquisition and retrieval. As a result, some of our most vivid memories might be our most inaccurate.

Memory, Emotion, and Identity

We are deeply emotional beings. Emotional memories, whether joyous or traumatic, tend to persist. As people approach the end of life, they revisit memories of childhood and early relationships. When one returns to an old home, what they miss isn't the place, but the self who lived there.

David Eagleman found that the brain uses more energy when encoding a novel experience. That's why first-time memories feel richer and more pleasurable to recall.

And yet, we often suffer from an insatiable appetite for memory accumulation. Some want to remember everything. But must we retain all that we come across?

Today, with unlimited external storage, our need for internal memory may be less—yet our anxiety about forgetting more. We read borrowed books while our own remain unread. We worry about memory loss, yet overlook what we already remember.

Isn't it a relief that some things fade?

The Necessity of Forgetting

A friend once told me that whenever he buys a new shirt, he discards an old one. Memory, too, demands such discipline.

We follow a "curve of forgetting": every new memory loosens the grip on the previous one. And yet, we try to hold on. Because without memory, the mind has no narrative. And without that narrative, we lose meaning.

The mind is not a perfect archive. It is a fabricated space—prone to gaps, rewrites, erasures, and embellishments. And yet, in this fragile construction lies our identity.

INTUITIVE MIND

Intuition is fast, effortless, associative, and slow learning. One wouldn't know where the insight emerged. Intuition is our gut feeling. Intuitive decisions are based on understanding, rather than on knowledge. Emotions are an integral part of intuition.

Intuition often outperforms rational analyses. Intuitions are often wrong because shortcuts sometimes lead to bias and sub-optimal decisions. The brain does a quick search of its stored files, finds an analogy with the present situation, and based on the knowledge; its meaning is ascribed.

Logic-based analysis, on the other hand, is slow, controlled, effortful, rule-governed, and emotionally neutral. On the other hand, intuitive decisions, even when based on pure guesswork, are often right. An interesting observation: "The trouble with intuition is that while intuitive modes of thought are easier to use than analytical modes, they are poorly adapted to many circumstances and decisions we face in the modern World."

For a decision, both intuition and reason are necessary. Reason enables us to go beyond mere perception, habit, and instinct. Intuition is an inference that is validated by the thinker's belief systems.

It is generally believed that reason-based decisions are better. We, however, know that many reason-based decisions have gone wrong. The reason is that we reason rather poorly. Our reasoning-based decision making is subjective. Our decisions fail due to irrational biases.

Decisions of skilled arguers often fail. The skilled arguers are not after the truth, but after arguments supporting their views. The result is that bias creeps in reasoning. It distorts evaluations and attitudes. We are good at 'biased reasoning'. We forget that, in order to pursue truth, the inputs of others are equally essential. We try to be both the judge and the advocate.

More objective reasoning is possible by developing abilities to distance oneself from one's own opinions, and consider other alternative opinions. We need to remember that all arguments are not debates (where the purpose is to win) but also producing arguments that are after the truth.

In order to learn how people make life-and-death decisions under extreme time pressure and uncertainty, Gary Klein talked to some fire-fighters. The firefighter told Klein that he couldn't think of a single decision he ever made. He said he just followed procedures. When Klein wanted to see the procedure manuals, the firefighter said, "It is not written down."

What Klein found was that the firefighter was not taking decisions in the classical sense. Before taking the decision, the firefighter did not generate a set of options, and then compared their pros and cons. Klein asked him a rephrased question. "How have you handled cases where you had struggled, cases where you might have made mistakes earlier in your career?"

The firefighter thus described one of his firefighting experiences. Since the smoke was coming from the back, the firefighter presumed it was probably a kitchen fire. He sent one of his crews inside the house to knock the fire out.

Klein asked the fireman why he sent a man inside the house when it is customary to go out of the house when a house is on fire. Why did he not break a window and use hoses to tame the fire?

The fireman told him that he did not do it because if he did that, he would have pushed the fire back into the house. This might have allowed it to spread wider into the house. Obviously, one wouldn't want to do that.

The fireman also told him that an interior attack is not always possible because if there is another house right next to it, it could also catch fire. In such cases, the firefighting starts externally.

Klein concludes, "You build up all these patterns, you quickly size up situations, and you know what to do. Experts know what to ignore, and what they have to watch carefully. Experts know what to expect next, so they get ready for that."

These are intuitive decisions. By intuition, Klein means the way we are able to use our experience. Intuition is not magic. It is based on experience. It allows us to build a repertoire of patterns that allows us to quickly frame situations, size situations up, and know what to do. It is not mere intuition, but intuition laced with mental simulation. Our mental simulation does the analysis. The decisions are primed by their ability to recognise situations balanced by the monitoring of mental simulation.

Intuition prepares us to see things that we couldn't see before. It gives us the ability to make fine distinctions. It helps us to better our pattern-recognition capabilities and alerts us to possible dangers.

"The intuitive mind is a sacred gift, and the rational mind is a faithful servant. We have created a society that honours the servant, and has forgotten the gift", Albert Einstein said years ago.

OVERBURDENED MIND

Fatigue sets in when we ask our minds to do more than they can manage. A tired mind clouds judgment. An overburdened mind often errs.

When decision fatigue strikes, we tend to do nothing, take shortcuts, and go wrong, or cling to the status quo.

We have a finite reserve of mental energy for exerting self-control. Willpower, like a muscle, weakens when used repeatedly over a short time.

Endless choices drain this energy. When willpower is depleted, we become cognitive misers—narrow, automatic, and one-dimensional in our thinking. While shopping, for instance, this makes us vulnerable—easy prey for marketers.

To preserve willpower, avoid temptations.

The harder the choices, the faster fatigue sets in. A fatigued decision-maker avoids judgment, favours ease, and takes the path of least resistance. But easy paths rarely lead to meaningful destinations. One of the easiest? Follow the seller's suggestion.

This challenge is magnified for the poor.

With less buying power and fewer options, the poor often reach satisfaction more quickly. Ironically, they may make more impulse purchases—despite limited means. These spontaneous choices reflect diminished self-control, not excess.

Decision fatigue and depleted willpower shape daily life—quietly, cumulatively. Every decision, big or small, chips away at our internal reserves. As willpower wanes, frustrations intensify. Ego-depleted people make illogical choices, favour short-term rewards, and may harm others just to make the easier choice.

The real danger? We rarely recognize when our willpower is low or our minds are fatigued.

We think we are always ready to decide.

But often, we are just reacting—automatically, unmindfully.

CHAOTIC MIND

The general belief is that our brain processes information through logical operations. However, chaos scientists challenge this view. They argue that the brain functions in unpredictable and nonlinear ways, and that the key to understanding it lies in chaos theory. According to them, the brain is a chaotic system, intricately regulated by internal feedback mechanisms.

One concept used to describe this chaotic behaviour is self-organised criticality. Such systems evolve naturally to a critical state without the need for fine-tuning of any external parameters. A classic example is a sandpile: as grains accumulate, the pile grows in a seemingly orderly way—until it reaches a tipping point and collapses. Each individual collapse may be unpredictable, but the overall distribution of collapses follows a regular pattern. This critical state sits right at the edge between stable, orderly behaviour and unpredictable chaos.

Disorder, it turns out, is vital to the brain's ability to transmit information and solve problems. Neuroscientists suggest that our brains operate in a "forest-on-fire" mode—one neuron ignites another, much like how a single burning tree can set others alight. Yet, just as not all trees catch fire at once, neural activity does not spread uniformly or continuously.

Experiments have shown that a single neuron can trigger a cascade of activity, resulting in bursts of collective firing followed by quieter periods—much like the rise and collapse of a sandpile. The brain often coordinates groups of neurons to fire together at the same frequency in a process known as phase locking. This allows different networks of neurons to communicate among themselves without interference from others. Yet, even within this order, instability creeps in—periods of synchronised activity can be disrupted, causing neurons to fire out of sync.

Interestingly, neurons that remain inactive for too long may die. Random firing of these idle neurons helps preserve their health. In this sense, a certain level of chaos in the brain is beneficial—it helps the body meet changing demands and fosters adaptability.

Chaotic brain activity is thought to play a central role in learning and the development of new abilities. Paradoxically, it is chaos that helps us organise our thoughts. What seems random is often part of a deeper order.

As Mark Twain famously noted, "It usually takes more than three weeks to prepare a good impromptu speech." Behind every spontaneous expression lies an intricate and chaotic yet strangely ordered process.

A MOTHER'S MIND

A little girl asks her mother, Ma, how did you live for so long without me?

I lived in anticipation, says the mother; In the anticipation of a bright tomorrow.

Ma, I know I am not the best. Yet, you say I am the best.

Mother's love is like the love a whole has for its parts. There is bias in mother's love. Mothers can't be too critical.

A mother is born the day her child is born.

The act of bringing someone into the world, and allowing them to begin their own journey demands courage and determination.

Who decides the right time for a mother to bring her child into the world?

Humans have unusually large brains relative to body size. If a baby were to remain in the womb any longer, its head might grow too large to pass safely through the birth canal. So, birth occurs when the brain has developed just enough to allow the baby to survive outside the womb.

A mother reaches a metabolic threshold around nine months, beyond which it becomes unsustainable to keep nourishing the growing foetus.

These nine months are not merely biological. They also give the mother time to bond with the life growing inside her, time to prepare, to dream, and to love.

It is the head size of the mother and the child that decides the right time for a mother to bring her child into the world.

Does a mother's love for her child depend upon birth pangs? Are adopting a child and giving birth to a child two different kinds of experiences? Is mother's love for her adopted child the same as her love for the child she gives birth to?

Behavioural neuroscientist Alison Fleming has been trying to find the answer to this question. Fleming wanted to understand how mothers think, how hormonal changes regulate mood, how cognition changes. She wanted to know what the long-term effects of mothering are.

Fleming says that the mother's dendrites (thread-like extensions of neurons that receive electrochemical stimulation) become more complex when she is interacting with her babies. She says amygdala is very important for mothering.

Does one need to give birth to become a mother?

Fleming says that mothering doesn't necessarily have to come from a mother. Fleming's studies showed that exposure to a baby over time can create the same mothering effect. Fleming says that any person who can raise a child is a mother. One needs to be sensitive and responsive.

One view says that the love for a non-biological child is not the same as the love one has for the child born out of one's own flesh and blood. Some adopters find the essence of connectedness missing in their relationship with the adopted child. Some say it takes years to develop real connectedness.

Is the quality of love in the two cases different? If they are different, is it due to genes? Does the adopted child need an additional measure of love to make up for the losses due to genes?

Many adopters say they are not sure if their love is different, but they feel their feelings are different. While others feel the quality of love between parents and nonbiological children has more chance of being better if the birth child arrives later than before.

Another view says that the parents who have already given birth are usually better placed to work at a relationship with a non-biological child because they have been through that. They say those who have their own baby and then decide to adopt a child, have different motivation for adopting a child.

There is yet another view that thinks those parents who have not experienced adoption have missed so much.

"You've missed the wonder of meeting a fully formed human being that is your child, complete with all the unspoken possibilities of that relationship."

Adoption of and giving birth to a child are two very different ways of building a relationship, just as establishing an organisation and acquiring an organisation are two different kinds of experiences.

The reality of life is that there is a difference between 'creating' and 'acquiring'. One is more like nature and the other is more like nurture. And as one adoptee says, "But I'm OK with that difference, and see it as part of my life story that's made me who I am."

Mother's love for her child is self-love. Conflict between a mother and her child is natural. The mother-child conflict starts unconsciously long before the child is born. This 'parent-offspring conflict', according to behavioural scientists, is due to the fact that mother does not want to give everything the child wants. The child wants to maximise its chance of survival and expects the mother to meet all the demands.

Nature has so beautifully resolved the unconscious mother-child conflict. It should not be difficult to resolve the conscious or unconscious conflict, if there is any, if there is understanding between the mother and the child that this conflict is natural.

The child may not need a mother's safety net, but they know that to fulfill their emotional requirement, there is no better place than the mother's lap.

Communication between a mother and her unborn child takes place through hormones (such as adrenaline, noradrenaline, and oxytocin), the child's behaviour (like the child's kicking in the womb), and the mother's love. The mother releases hormones when under stress. In moderation, these hormones stimulate a child's neural and psychological systems beneficially, but in excess they can affect the child adversely (like low birth weight, reading difficulties, behaviour problems, and gastric disorders).

The mother's love, acceptance, and positive thoughts play a very important role in the development of the foetus. The unborn child appears to get strongly affected by the mother's negative or ambivalent attitude toward the pregnancy.

The most traumatic experience the unborn child faces is when, for some reason, the mother withdraws her love and support from the child. Withdrawal of love and affection for the child during pregnancy may lead to the birth of a depressed child.

A stressful relationship between the mother and the father also affects the child. A father who abuses or neglects his pregnant wife can affect a child, both emotionally and physically. An anxiety-ridden mother can leave a deep scar on the personality of the developing foetus. Likewise, a self-assured and confident mother instils in the child a deep sense of content and security.

For nurturing proper understanding between the two human beings, an open and inviting space is essential.

This fundamental human understanding adequately explains the bond between a mother and her child. The mother-child bonding that begins prenatally is vital even after the birth. Empathy with the child and the ability to see things from a child's perspective are key factors that stimulate mother-child bond.

Mother knows the child much before the child is born. She has tools to make her child a happy child. The tools are her thoughts and feelings. During the gestation period, the foetus senses the comforting maternal heartbeat. It is the child's main source of life, safety, and love. Mother's steady heartbeat reassures the child that all is well.

Responsibilities of parenthood are immense. According to a study, supportive parents provide reassurance to their child, offer their child a strategy for coping with their distress, show affection, and encourage their child to wait patiently.

Scientists say that mothers can be brain enhancers. Maternal support in early childhood, predicted the studies, larger hippocampal volumes at school age. The hippocampus, a part of the brain, is strongly associated with forming, connecting, organizing, and storing memories. Hippocampus' size has been linked to the capacity to manage stress.

Studies have found that preschool-age children whose mothers actively support them during a stressful incident later show greater volume in the hippocampus. The studies indicate that kids who receive warm, supportive parenting are better at coping with adversity and at completing cognitive tasks later in life. The positive effect of maternal support on hippocampal volumes was observed to be greater in non-depressed children.

Mother-child bonding isn't just for brains, it is also an affair of the heart.

The heart cells not only contract and expand rhythmically to pump blood, they also communicate with fellow cells. Perhaps this is why most mothers instinctively place their babies close to their hearts.

Scientific evidence indicates that a mother's heart stimulates a newborn's heart, thereby activating a dialogue between the infant's brain, mind, and heart. This heart-to-heart communication helps the mother too. It activates dormant intelligence in the mother. This is nature's way of keeping a mother's intelligence awake.

Touch is necessary for human development. During the critical period of development following birth, the infant brain undergoes a massive growth of neural connections. Synaptic connections in the cortex continue to proliferate. At about two years, they peak. During this period, one of the most crucial things to survival and healthy development is touch. All mothers know this instinctively.

Newborns are born expecting to be held, handled, cuddled, rubbed, kissed. "In nature's nativity scene, mother's arms have always been a baby's bed, breakfast, transportation, even entertainment."

The fundamental bond between a mother and a child is the result of an ongoing conversation conducted on multiple levels, from the physiological to the emotional, cognitive, and social. The mother-child bonding is influenced by the smell, the skin-to-skin contact, the facial expressions, eye movements, body language, the kissing, the cooing, the cuddling, the tone of the mother's voice, and the baby talk.

There is nothing like mother's milk.

This watery thing is the mother's pride. It changes its composition to satisfy the needs of the child. The nutritious liquid that a mother produces for her newborn child is a source of all nutrition, emotional gratification, and a sense of fulfilment. Mother's milk can't be replicated.

As Oliver Wendell Holmes said, "A pair of substantial mammary glands has the advantage over the two hemispheres of the most learned professor's brain in the art of compounding a nutritious fluid for infants."

The Darwinian theory of evolution suggests that infant feeding should benefit both the mother and the child. In other words, "an infant should be breastfed as much as possible to maximise its chances of survival, whereas a mother must balance her current metabolic investment in milk production with her potential investment in future offspring".

MIND AND MONEY

Money is essential for survival. Freedom, desire, power, status, work, and possession—the forces that shape life—almost always revolve around money. And yet, money-making doesn't appeal to all. Nor is everyone able to make money.

It is often said that to make money, one must possess a certain degree of stupidity and greed. But it isn't always greed that makes us addicted to money. The obsession can stem from the desire for status or the need to compensate for social insecurities.

Thinking about money alters the way we think. To understand money-related anxieties, we must ask: Why is money important to us? How much do we truly need to achieve what matters? What is the best way to acquire it? And what are our economic responsibilities to others in the process?

A rich man doesn't know what to do with money. A poor man doesn't know what to do without it. We suffer from money illusion. We gladly accept a 7% salary hike during 11% inflation, but resist a 4% pay cut in a year with zero inflation. We are trapped by loss aversion, reacting more strongly to losses than to equivalent gains. Money gives us instant pleasure when gained, and disproportionate pain when lost. It nudges us toward self-centeredness.

Opportunities to make easy money activate surges of dopamine in our neural circuits. We value money we earn more than money we are given. Yet money often erodes relationships. When social norms and market norms are kept apart, life flows smoothly. But when they collide, complications arise.

We can't ignore money. But we must train the mind to separate the pleasure of purchase from the pain of payment. Those with neither assets nor liabilities may be closer to achieving this balance.

Money enables us to buy things, but it also distracts us from simple, everyday joys. It can compensate for social rejection and reduce discomfort, but it can also distance us from life's subtler pleasures. Material wants require a fixed sum, but happiness is relative: it hinges not on what we have, but on how our earnings compare with our neighbours'. Escaping this relativity trap is not easy.

We also suffer from blind foresight. Our efforts are governed by the magnitude of rewards we expect. Yet, motivations are not always conscious—we often act without understanding what drives us.

WHERE THE MIND IS WITHOUT FEAR

Rabindranath Tagore rightly said that the head can be held high only when the mind is without fear.

Yet fear is not easy to forget. Threats linger. Accidents haunt us. If one has met with a mishap while driving at night, the very idea of night driving may later seem dreadful. Fearful memories return easily—and are hard to shake off.

Fear is a natural part of the human psyche. It is adaptive. Fear conditioning helps us learn how to anticipate and respond to threats. Our early human ancestors survived because they were quick to react to danger. Obstacles trained our brains to sense and escape harm.

Fear is often tied to the instinct to escape or avoid. In moments of fear, we fight, freeze, or flee. In less than 100 milliseconds, sensory signals reach the amygdala. In a split second, adrenaline surges. Eyes widen, heart rate quickens, breath becomes rapid, stomach churns, palms sweat, and time seems to slow down—these are the classic signs of fear.

The amygdala, the brain's fear center, triggers these responses. When the amygdala is deactivated, both the learning and expression of fear can be disrupted.

We experience many kinds of fear: fear of death, fear of the unknown, fear of being alone, fear of the future, fear of failure, and more. Paradoxically, fear holds the key to survival. Without it, perhaps, we would not have endured as a species. Evolution favoured those who feared the right things at the right time.

Fear involves unconscious autonomic responses arising from various parts of the brain. The thalamus, our brain's relay station, filters and forwards only the most crucial sensory information. The sensory cortex interprets these signals. The hippocampus stores and retrieves memory. The amygdala decodes emotions, assesses threats, and archives fear-laden memories. Finally, the hypothalamus orchestrates the fear response, triggering two distinct but simultaneous pathways.

The low road is quick and instinctive—it shoots first, asks questions later.

The high road is thoughtful and deliberate—it evaluates options before responding.

Both eventually converge at the hypothalamus, which activates the body's fear response through the sympathetic nervous system and the adrenal-cortical system. Together, they produce the full-blown expression of fear.

Humans also have the unique capacity to anticipate. Anticipating danger can provoke the same physiological response as the danger itself—sometimes even more intensely. This anticipatory fear, while distressing, can also prepare us.

People with a damaged amygdala may be incapable of fear. But does the absence of fear make one brave?

Should we sacrifice the amygdala to become fearless?

TEENAGER'S MIND

The foundational years of life, from birth to age five, are crucial. During this period, a child's linguistic and cognitive abilities grow rapidly. Emotional, social, and moral capacities also begin to take root. Literacy and numeracy skills are shaped in these early years, and any emotional impairment can have deep, lasting impacts.

Parents play a pivotal role at this stage. A loving home environment not only enriches a child's vocabulary but also fosters emotional security. Conversely, family violence or an unsafe neighbourhood can have damaging effects. The bond between grandparents and grandchildren is especially powerful; research shows that children cared for by grandparents often fare better than those in costly daycare settings.

Adolescence, however, is a different terrain altogether. It is not a simple continuation of childhood. It is a phase of becoming—when identities are formed, risks are taken, and truths are tested. Teenagers start discovering the world on their own terms. It is a time of paradoxes: bold experimentation coexists with emotional vulnerability. It is the age when peer pressure peaks, self-awareness intensifies, and mental health challenges often emerge—anxiety, depression, addictions, eating disorders.

The teenage brain undergoes massive reorganization from ages 12 to 25. This period of heightened brain plasticity enables rapid learning, but also leaves teens more susceptible to external stressors. Neuroscience tells us the brain operates on a "use it or lose it" principle: active neural connections are strengthened, while unused ones are pruned away. Interestingly, different age groups may rely on different brain circuits and cognitive strategies to solve the same problem. While adults often lean on societal norms, adolescents tend to trust their instincts and personal experience.

Teenagers may possess sharp intellects, yet they often struggle to channel them effectively. In calm settings, they can reason almost like adults, but stress can hijack their decision-making. The emotional brain overpowers the rational brain.

Parents often flood their teens with advice about study habits, focus, and discipline. But the line between guiding and controlling is delicate. Research suggests that when parents adopt a light yet consistent guiding hand and respect their children's need for independence, teens thrive.

Hurriedly cramming a young mind is like speed-packing a flimsy suitcase. It may hold, but only temporarily. Quick learners might retain information for a while, but unless the learning is layered, integrated, and paced, it won't last. A carefully and gradually packed neural suitcase preserves its contents far better—and prepares the mind for deeper understanding. In the end, the harder something is to recall, the harder it is to forget.

THE RAY MIND

The mind of Satyajit Ray was a rare confluence of multiple intelligences—cinematic, literary, musical, graphic, and philosophical. Here are a few distilled aspects that sketch the contours of his extraordinary mind.

Ray had the eye of a documentarian and the soul of a poet. He noticed the subtle rhythms of everyday life, capturing gestures, silences, and atmospheres that others overlooked.

Deeply rooted in Bengali culture and yet cosmopolitan, Ray combined Rabindranath Tagore's humanism with the visual language of Western masters like Renoir and Kurosawa. His mind was not divided—it was woven.

As a trained graphic designer and illustrator, Ray thought in images. His films were often storyboarded like paintings. His mind saw the film before it was made.

Whether it was a child's longing, a woman's quiet strength, or a failed zamindar's decay, Ray could step into the skin of others. His mind was empathetically cinematic.

There was precision in Ray's process. From composing music to designing typefaces to editing frames, he approached each detail with the rigor of a scientist and the curiosity of a child.

Ray did not shout. But his critiques of modernity, of class, gender, and colonial residues, were sharp, layered, and subversive. His mind resisted all reduction.

He was a filmmaker, but also a writer of detective and sci-fi stories, a composer, a calligrapher, and a publisher. The Ray mind, a constellation of many stars.

THE BLIND MIND

Andha Yug, Dharamvir Bharati's landmark play, set in the aftermath of the Mahabharata war, was written in the years following the Partition of India. It speaks not just of the destruction of human lives, but also of the collapse of ethical values. In the Mahabharata, both the victor and the vanquished ultimately lose.

In The Country of the Blind, H.G. Wells tells a tale of stagnation. A mountaineer, by accident, stumbles into a hidden valley cut off from the world, inhabited entirely by blind people. Though self-sufficient, the villagers are insular and resistant to new ideas. They have no concept of sight and dismiss it as delusion. Even the woman the mountaineer loves cannot grasp the idea of vision. His "unstable obsession with sight" is viewed as a sign of mental illness. Eventually, the villagers decide that the mountaineer must be cured by removing his eyes. He chooses to flee.

Sight can be confusing. Brian Friel, drawing from a case history by Oliver Sacks, explores this theme in a poignant story. A woman born blind gains sight in midlife. But the world she sees bewilders her. She cannot make sense of forms, spaces, or distances. The clarity she hoped for never arrives. Overwhelmed, she longs to return to the familiarity of blindness.

Blindness has served as a rich metaphor across literature. Bharati uses it to represent the dehumanisation of the individual and society. Wells portrays it as a symbol of social restriction and the suppression of individuality. Friel—and Sacks—

suggest that sight, far from being a straightforward gift, can also disorient and isolate. José Saramago, in Blindness, extends the metaphor further to depict not just personal misfortune, but social breakdown and moral catastrophe.

In 'blind' times, we look for icons—figures who can help us navigate the darkness. We yearn for torchbearers to lead us out of the tunnel.

A WINNER'S MIND

To be fitter than the other is the usual mantra to win a race.

But fitness is contextual. One person may be fitter in one trait or in one environment; another may thrive in a different context. A true winner becomes the fittest in their trait and their environment. A winner knows the ways of winning. It has to be her/his day.

How do we ascertain if someone possesses the qualities to become an effective mass leader?

We expect them to understand the needs of an open system. We expect them to handle the complexities and expectations of large, diverse social groups.

The dynamics between a leader and their followers are changing. A political brain today is an emotional brain. People make decisions with their feelings—emotions matter. In this context, heredity and caste can't be ignored.

Winners understand that responsibility is as important as freedom. The more freedom they enjoy, the more responsibility they must bear. Unlimited freedom is as undesirable as imposed social responsibility. Freedom enables growth—but unchecked, it can also increase social disorder. Responsibility balances that disorder, anchoring stability.

Responsibility is not a 'detachable burden', nor a 'popularity contest'. The duties of the winner do not end with the end of a battle.

Yet, too often, people take on or are assigned responsibilities disproportionate to their capabilities. There is a need to restrain this enthusiasm—both in assuming and delegating responsibility.

It is easier to propagate a principle than to practice it. Particularly in public life, courage is needed even more than vigilance.

If we have the right to freedom, we have the obligation to respect others' freedom.

If we have the right to security, we must help ensure conditions for all to feel secure.

If we have the right to education, we must learn to our fullest and share our knowledge.

If we have the right to participate in democracy, we must ensure the best are chosen.

Choosing the right winners is our collective responsibility.

It is also our duty to periodically monitor the conduct and commitment of our leaders. They may act freely to pursue their ends, but we must remind them: we are not invisible, even if they refuse to see us; we cannot be made invisible, even if they turn a blind eye.

Kaushik Basu cautions: "If you lack talent, cultivate power. This will attract fawners around you, and you will never again know you don't have talent."

Michel Foucault viewed power as both enabling and constraining.

The powerful often forget that power is a responsibility. But those who truly understand power know that it is not a burden—they recognize the value of restraint.

The powerful cannot afford to be pretend-sleepers when it's time to act.

And the followers cannot afford to tolerate such sleepers in positions of responsibility.

Too often, the powerful become so self-absorbed that they believe only they have the right to do wrong. They misuse power, assuming rules apply only to the commoners. They treat it as an insult when treated as equals.

But power is not poison—unless one is attached to it.

True winners know that the power they are entrusted with is meant to empower others.

They respect the responsibility of the chair they sit on.

What matters more: competence or trust?

Evolutionary psychologist Jacob Vigil says it depends on how much power the other has to help or harm. Those who've faced life's challenges tend to value trust and care.

Those who haven't faced significant obstacles tend to be more competence-oriented.

It is our responsibility to ensure that winners don't get the chance to manipulate us.

We need trustworthy leadership.

Real winners know that one way to maximize their payoff is to ensure others get their due. They understand that equality of opportunity is not enough—efficiency often determines the winner.

Real victors understand the meaning of victory. They care for the dreams and struggles of ordinary people. They can distinguish between hope and hype.

In a democracy, disagreement is not a bad word. And not every opponent is malevolent.

A winner is in a precarious situation when there is no opposition.

Ayn Rand aptly described this predicament:

"The question isn't who is going to let me; it's who is going to stop me."

If no one is there to stop me, it becomes my bounden duty to stop myself.

If I must lead, I must also know how to follow.

Politics is noble when rooted in public service.

IS GOD A CONSTRUCT OF THE MIND?

Some say God is the creator of something from nothing. Others say God is belief itself: hope beyond reason. But why must God be all-knowing and all-powerful? What if God is less godlike?

We create God in our own image. Our expectations shape the God we worship. There are always good reasons—to believe, and to disbelieve.

Einstein's God didn't reward or punish. He saw in the universe a deep, almost religious awe—beyond morality, beyond doctrine.

Tagore's God was unknowable, beyond reach. Neither personal nor punitive, he did not dwell in a distant heaven. He was present—in every corner of the world, in the songs Tagore sang, in the lonely streets he walked. For him, God was Absolute Existence—desireless, detached, silent. And yet, necessary. "Without the world, God would be a phantasm; without God, the world would be chaos."

Leon Lederman writes: "In the very beginning, there was a void... a nothingness containing no space, no time, no matter. Yet the laws of nature were in place. Only God knows what happened at the very beginning."

Richard Dawkins insists the only watchmaker is blind physics. He calls belief in God a scientific question.

Francis Collins replies: if it is a scientific question, then science must provide the tools to answer it.

Charles Darwin once observed: "If a solution, consistent with the ordinary course of nature, can be found, we must not invoke an abnormal act of Creative Power."

Simple logic says: something survives if it is advantageous. Faith in God must have served some purpose. God would not have endured if he hadn't proven useful—emotionally, socially, psychologically.

We may doubt the existence of God, yet we often behave as though we believe in something—by whatever name we call it. The illusion of God is nearly universal. The sense that someone is watching is deeply ingrained in us. God, whether real or not, functions.

Maybe God is an evolved projection of what we think God ought to be—a mirror of our fears, longings, and hopes. And as long as he remains useful, we will continue to believe him.

MIND IS OUR FIRST BATTLEFIELD

To win a war, one must first win the war within.

Wars are first fought with doubts, desires, and decisions. A glance, a gesture, a pause can achieve what swords cannot.

In the Mahabharata, Yudhishthira is bound by dharma, yet his unyielding commitment to truth becomes a vulnerability. Krishna bends morality to serve a higher cause.

Krishna's diplomacy, his moral ambiguities, his use of logic and emotional intelligence to shape events—these reveal the immense psychological, ethical, and strategic depths of the epic.

The Bhagavad Gita is a battlefield of doubt, surrender, and awakening. The dice game is not mere chance—it is the ultimate psychological warfare. Draupadi's interrogation of Dharma is a strategic challenge. Karna's inner turmoil is a war of loyalty against moral truth.

Sometimes, ethical manipulation becomes necessary in pursuit of a larger truth.

To prevent a greater harm, one may mislead.

Deception, in the right hands, becomes morally permissible—even essential.

In such moments, strategy outweighs sincerity.

Mind games—whether to probe, provoke, or pacify—require as much psychological insight as ideological clarity.

In both Mahabharata and Ramayana, wars are won in moments of hesitation, in whispered counsel. Real diplomacy lives there—between dharma and deception, in the silent terrain of the mind.

The Ramayana is not simply a clash between good and evil. It unfolds in complex emotional landscapes—where duty, power, love, and ego collide beneath the surface.

Manthara poisons Kaikeyi's mind with insecurity. Ravana's deceptions lure Sita through disguise and psychological bait.

Vibhishana's conflict is not external—it is a war between loyalty and righteousness.

His rebellion is quiet, a game of intellect and conscience. In Lanka, Hanuman uses subtle tactics to unnerve the enemy—his fire is not just flame, but fear. Rama's occasional silence is calculated—each pause, a Dharma-laden strategy. His calm acceptance of exile is an emotional masterstroke, disarming opposition with dignity.

Diplomacy is the most recognized mind game.

Here silence speaks louder than declarations.

Perception often outweighs truth. From ancient civilizations to modern corridors of power, the diplomat remains a master of restraint, not spectacle.

A diplomat knows when to speak, when to remain silent, and when to ask. They read the eyes before the lips. Ethics, for them, are not fixed codes but adaptable masks.

A diplomat carries both peace offerings and silent warnings. Their words must comfort one side, confuse another, and conceal their true intent from both.

In diplomacy, what is not said often holds more power than what is said.

MIND WORKS BEST IN THE BATHROOM

Reflection and creativity often thrive in moments of pause and movement — in the mundane. Bathrooms and buses become sites of unlikely epiphanies, unburdened by urgency or expectation, for thoughts to pop up.

A fish in a pond near a railway track grows faster. Not because of superior water or food, but perhaps because of motion - subtle, involuntary, rhythmic - prompted by the vibrations of passing trains.

And in that unplanned, repetitive movement lies a secret: growth. Motion awakens the body, sharpens the senses, and alters the rhythm.

Like the fish, often we grow, not by logic, but by vibration.

The mind that can see in the mirror a window does not stop at the immediate reflection of the outer self. It looks into the silent presence of everything that surrounds the reflected self. The mirror, to such a mind, is not a tool for vanity but a portal of perception.

When you look into a mirror, you see the trace of a recent joy, the mark of a burden not yet shed. The mirror becomes a frame for both the individual and the invisible relationships that define you. The mirror reminds you that you are never alone in your image.

Your surroundings, your context, your memories—they follow you into the frame.

To see a window in the mirror is to recognize that reflection is not isolation. It is connection. It is awareness. It is the merging of inner and outer worlds.

As long as we have time to go to the bathroom and travel in a bus, we shall remain bioengineering marvels.

A BORROWED MIND

What is it that we truly want? We say one thing, mean another, and act in contradiction to both. What we want is often a shadow, fleeting, context-bound.

Where Is the problem if we don't know what we want?

Perhaps there is no problem. Perhaps not knowing gives us mystery, momentum. Desire undefined keeps us seeking. Unclear wants lead us to stories, to depth, to paths we never planned, to people we never imagined, to parts of ourselves we didn't know existed.

Perhaps, the problem is in our craving for clarity when life itself thrives in ambiguity.

There are many who do not know what they want, not because they are lost, but because they are used; used by the hour, by the job, by the demands of others. Their lives are scheduled by necessity, their breaths owned by

obligation. They don't know what makes them happy.
They have families they barely see, mirrors they no
longer face. They live in borrowed time. Every moment
filled by someone else's need.

They are not aimless. They move with great purpose.
But the purpose is not their own.

Perhaps the real tragedy is not that they do not know
what they want, but that they have never asked
themselves what they want.

If all our time is borrowed, where is the room for
freedom?

Freedom begins in the ability to stop, step back, and
wonder. On borrowed time, freedom is not a right.

Some don't want to make freedom a forgotten luxury.
Some are bound by duty, to understand what freedom
is.

MARITAL MINDS

Marital relationships often grow stale over time. The
prime reasons are gradual erosion of novelty and
emotional intimacy. What begins as a vibrant
connection falter under the weight of routine, unspoken
grievances, or unmet expectations. Familiarity, though
comforting, can also breed neglect; partners may take

each other for granted, focusing on obligations rather than nurturing the relationship.

Communication often suffers as years pass. Couples stop sharing their dreams, fears, or even mundane details of their day. Emotional withdrawal creates an invisible chasm between two people who once promised to navigate life together. External pressures—work, financial stress, parenting—add to this, pushing the relationship further into stagnation.

Conflicts in marital relationships often arise not from the present but from the shadows of the past. Even when two people come from similar families—same class, same culture—their experiences within those families can differ profoundly, shaping how they view the world and, by extension, their partner.

Each individual carries an invisible suitcase filled with the values, habits, and expectations instilled in them during their formative years. One may have grown up in a home where silence signalled respect, while the other equates silence with indifference. One might see money as something to be saved; the other, as something to be enjoyed. Neither is wrong, but these differences can ignite conflict when unexamined or misunderstood.

Then there are past experiences—previous relationships, disappointments, even childhood memories—that colour how each partner reacts to love and conflict. A small disagreement can escalate, not because of the issue at hand, but because of unresolved emotions rooted in the past.

Even in families with similar social status, the dynamics of upbringing differ. A seemingly minor gesture—like how one expresses gratitude or addresses elders—can stir emotions when it doesn't align with the partner's expectations. Over time, these differences accumulate, creating friction that neither fully understands.

The challenge, then, is to recognize these influences and confront them together. A successful marriage requires not just love, but also the willingness to unpack those suitcases, to understand the weight of what the other carries, and to find ways to walk forward without tripping over the baggage.

It is not about erasing the past but about integrating it into a shared future, learning to honour each other's differences while forging a new path together. Only when partners commit to this journey of mutual understanding can they transform conflict into growth and stagnation into renewal.

Who can revive such relationships? They themselves. Recognizing the drift is the first step. Once acknowledged, communicate honestly: Rebuild the habit of empathetic conversations. Set aside time for each other, away from distractions. Rediscover shared interests. Acknowledge that both have grown and changed over time. Embrace this evolution rather than resist it.

Professionals provide tools and techniques to navigate conflicts, rebuild trust, and deepen intimacy. Trusted individuals can offer advice, though care must be taken to respect boundaries. Outside agencies can guide and facilitate, but the willingness to change must come from the couple themselves. Ultimately, the most sustainable revival comes from within.

A HUMOROUS MIND

Humour is both universal and uniquely personal. It is often contagious.

What makes us laugh? Why are things funny?

Humour is said to have a cognitive cleanup mechanism and is intimately linked to our thinking process. Brain scientists have shown that puns and other types of jokes are deciphered in different regions of the brain. They found activation in an area of the brain called the medial prefrontal cortex when jokes are processed. This area controls our reward-related behaviour.

We are unique because of our perceptual and intellectual ability. Humour encourages this ability.

Humour occurs when the brain recognises a pattern that surprises it, and recognition of this sort is rewarded with the experience of the humour response.

Our brains daily observations are dependent on several assumptions, and incomplete information. The brain has to complete the task of anticipating the future in a world that is unfolding at a fast pace. Under the circumstances, mistakes are inevitable.

"We do a quick and dirty assessment and make a lot of best guesses. But this fills our mental spaces with junk, small mistakes that could trigger a cascade of errors if they go undetected, leading us to waste a lot of energy and resources and, in the worst case, inviting disaster."

Finding the errors and then disabling them is not easy. Our brain has to do this job, in addition to myriad other competing jobs. Basically, the brain has to bribe itself to do this important work.

Humour arose when our long-ago ancestors were furnished with open-ended thinking. The process of natural selection was not enough to order our brain to find and fix all our mistakes. The brain was needed to be 'bribed' with pleasure. This wired-in source of pleasure has made us addicted to humour.

A joke or a cartoon can raise our spirits. We laugh from sudden feelings of superiority over other people. We laugh because laughter gives us relief by releasing pent-up psychic energy. Laugh during a stressful situation are often helpful in reducing the stress.

Economist Kaushik Basu's once remarked about powerful people. The powerful have no way of knowing if they have a sense of humour because ordinary people will always laugh at their jokes.

If the genesis of humour is analysed too vigorously, it gets ruined.

"The most common kind of joke is that in which we expect one thing and another is said; here our own disappointed expectation makes us laugh."

Humour is especially effective when people laugh at themselves. We often become fools in order to prove ourselves wise. Laughing at others gives one joy, but there is also joy at being laughed at.

We all have acoustically distinctive laughter. Laughter follows norms and customs of the society. Laughter does not imply only humour. Laughter gives instant relief from hopeless situations.

Laughing is a ticklish matter. We don't laugh if someone slips on a banana peel and breaks his leg, but we laugh if he slips and gets up immediately.

It is common to use laughter as a friction dampener among warring factions. Laughter can likewise function to mitigate problems or social ambivalence within a group.

Laughter can be induced and there are 'qualified' laughter inducers. Laughter can also be induced chemically.

Humour is our unique ability. Our brains are hardwired for laughter. We may take the help of laughter in situations when we are in uncomfortable situations. There is 'nervous laughter'.

Humour can be quite demanding to the brain. Humour triggers a precise repertoire of responses: the order, timing, and emphasis must be just right; irrelevant or distracting elements must be discounted or ignored.

The job of a comedian is to entertain people. But it can take a personal toll on his or her mental health. Some comedians have described their act "very dangerous, like walking a tightrope, or like running across a lake of ice where the ice is breaking behind you and it is going to take an hour to get to the other side."

The worst thing for a comedian is to find no one laughing at their jokes.

Jokes are often hierarchical. One is expected to laugh at the boss's jokes, whether one finds them funny or not.

It is not easy to hold a laugh, and as Stephen King said, "You can't deny laughter; when it comes, it plops down in your favourite chair and stays as long as it wants.

HOBAY NA

Some people are always ready to lodge complaints, armed with reasons why they cannot do the work assigned to them. For them, obstacles are not challenges to overcome but justifications to remain stagnant.

Scepticism and cynicism contribute to the "Hobay Na" culture. Scepticism questions feasibility but can also lead to constructive criticism. If scepticism turns into chronic doubt, it fuels inertia. Cynicism dismisses efforts outright. It discourages initiative and reinforces a culture of inaction.

 "Hobay Na" is also shaped by systemic inefficiencies, lack of accountability, bureaucratic hurdles. It's a mix of mindset and environment.

Hobay Na reflects a habit. Bureaucratic hurdles and false promises may be common everywhere, but in some places, they become excuses rather than challenges to overcome.

Some people take pride in defiance. They "understand" before even trying to understand, assuming they already know the outcome. It's a mindset where refusal to act is seen as a mark of experience.

Conformation to work ethic is highly infectious. The same person who resists work in one place might become otherwise in another.

Among Bengalis, there exists a peculiar cultural duality: on the one hand, the resigned, almost instinctive "Hobay Na"—"It won't work"—and on the other, the expansive, unhurried spirit of Adda, those winding, open-ended conversations that shape lives as much as they evade solutions.

At first glance, Hobay Na seems defeatist. It rejects proposals, punctures ambition. But this attitude is not merely cynicism; it is a form of rigorous scepticism born of a long history—colonial subjugation, the burden of inherited intellect, and the disillusionments of modernity. In Bengal, intelligence was cultivated early, but power was not. Perhaps Hobay Na is the child of this mismatch.

Adda, meanwhile, ripens in the same eastern climate—humid, slow, and reflective. It is not small talk. It is digressive thinking, democratic space, collective remembering. It occurs in tea stalls, verandas, college canteens, and even within bureaucratic boredom. In Adda, ideas are examined, not executed. Here, Hobay Na is not a dead end but a pause—a way of saying, "Let us speak of this first."

While other cultures possess similar form, what makes Bengal distinct is the deep entanglement between resistance and reflection, between inertia and imagination. Adda becomes not a waste of time but time's reimagination.

Perhaps this is why ideas in Bengal are often born prematurely, lived richly in conversation, and rarely pursued to completion. It is not because Bengalis cannot act, but because the act is forever being rehearsed in thought. It is a culture where the prototype is enough, and the perfect plan can always wait until tomorrow.

Hobay Na lives side by side with Adda. One questions the world's feasibility; the other, its meaning. In that tension, a culture breathes.

THE MIND OF A BUTTERFLY

Some come into this world with a mindset to spread colour. Their very presence lifts spirits and brings good humour. They brighten the lives of those around them, like a colourful butterfly.

Butterflies, once repulsive caterpillars, emerge graceful and beautiful, like living flowers. They cannot fly straight, but they know how to live. Though their moments are brief, they think that is enough.

Rabindranath said, "They flutter for a day and think it is forever."

We often consider something valuable only if it has economic worth. But time spent on pursuits that seem uneconomical is not always wasted. What appears "useless" may offer a different kind of fulfilment.

A butterfly may have no weight, but it understands the value of leisure.

Then there are the silkworms. A silkworm works relentlessly, day and night, spinning silk — something with clear cash value. Silkworm-minded people understand only this kind of value. They have little time

to nurture their softer side, or to savour the new colours
of life.

But even the silkworm minds must learn from the
butterflies: bringing sunshine into others' lives is never
a waste of time, because it brings sunshine into their
own lives, too.

THE MIND OF A STAR

Some people enjoy a privileged existence. Some inherit
it, others create it. Some are even able to create their
luck. They may not be extraordinarily talented, but they
know how to maximise whatever talent they possess.
They have the ability to get along with others. They are
ambitious. They know how to accept failure
intelligently.

It is often believed that only those who deserve success
achieve it. But this is not always true. Nor is it true that
only the hardworking succeed. Success doesn't always
demand sacrifice or compromise. Some people get
more than they deserve.

The X-factors of success—charisma, chutzpah, joie de
vivre, and grace—are not equally distributed. Some
possess these in abundance.

The minds of certain stars radiate these X-factors. They
are sharp and witty. They enjoy making fun of others
but don't like being the target of jokes. They know how
to be brash or gentle, depending on what the situation

demands. They are excellent communicators, endowed with a rare combination of expressivity, sensitivity, control, eloquence, vision, and self-confidence. Their verbal fluency is laced with wit and charm. They instinctively know what might interest another person, especially their female admirers.

They succeed because they can envision their success. They are aware of both their charisma and their flaws. They rarely challenge conventions, yet remain popular despite their audacious behaviour. They dislike criticism. Naturally provocative, they possess the boldness to push boundaries. They are spirited, and their passionate exuberance is their forte.

The good thing about exuberance is that it is contagious. It spreads quickly and expands people's sense of possibility. Some star minds know how to make others feel important. People envy them. One may not like them, but they are impossible to ignore.

Magician Steve Cohen once unlocked the secret to influence, charisma, and showmanship when he said:

"The trick itself is never important; it's having a presentational hook."

Star minds know that charisma is more about image than innate ability.

Let their star power not overshadow the substance within.

A STRAIGHT MIND

The shortest distance between two points is a straight line, but we often fail to follow this simple geometrical instruction. What are the possible temptations that direct us to take routes that are not straight?

Our desires are always greater than our necessities. We are always eager to fulfil our desires that we forget what line or curve we are following to fulfil those desires. Economic compulsion is one of the major reasons that lead us to take not so straight lines. Some of us can't resist the temptation of making bad money.

Niccolo Machiavelli said, "Men are so simple and so ready to obey present necessities that one who deceives will always find those who allow themselves to be deceived."

We all love to put in the least efforts to achieve the maximum. There is nothing wrong if one follows the law of least effort. In majority of cases, we get cheated because we want to follow shortcuts. We get cheated because we want to get cheated. We become, knowingly or unknowingly, willing partners of the cheating process. The situational contingencies lead us to behave inconsistently.

We all like to behave like idealists. But when we come nearer to the problem, we falter, especially when the problem affects us personally.

John Galsworthy said, "Idealism increases in direct proportion to one's distance from the problem."

Robert Thouless has given a few helpful guru mantras for walking on not-so-straight line. These include: use emotionally toned words and gestures to get undue attention, emphasise the trivial and ignore the important to let down an opponent, contradict and misrepresent an opponent's position by diverting his attention to irrelevant issues, point out the logical correctness of the form of an argument whose premises contain doubtful or untrue statements of fact, use of pseudo-technical jargon to confidently present false credentials, use questions to draw out damaging admissions, angering an opponent deliberately so that he argues badly, and so on.

Creating controversy is another kind of crooked thinking. Arthur Schopenhauer's strategies of controversy include: claim victory despite defeat; interrupt, break, divert the dispute; meet the opponent with a counterargument as bad as his, make him exaggerate his statement, appeal to authority rather than reason; and so on.

It is handy to remember that straight-line solutions are not possible if problems are bigger than logic. It is difficult to teach a crab to walk straight. So beware of the crabs. If that is not possible, learn the ways of the crabs.

A SHY MIND

Shyness is an essential part of our psyche. It becomes evident on our faces and in our deeds that we don't want to talk about this 'odd state of mind'. One can observe it in our heartbeats or upset stomachs.

Shyness must have benefited us; otherwise, it would not have existed, evolutionarily speaking. From a survival standpoint, perhaps, shyness has an evolutionary advantage.

There was a time when shyness was not that evident. One lived far more in public; whole families would eat, sleep, and socialise together in the same room. Shyness increases as the possibilities of human contact and interaction decrease.

We are not shy in certain situations. We feel shy when we are talking to a stranger. In the presence of some strangers, we feel threatened and try to protect ourselves from the perceived threat. Because of the perceived threat, we feel inferior to that person, and if the person is 'attractive', we feel even more threatened. We become more concerned about this person's thinking and how to deal with it. As a result, we struggle to communicate. We try to avoid eye contact.

Are introverts shy people?

Introverts prefer solitude to social activities. Shy people long for contacts with other people, but feel awkward and fearful to make such contacts.

Shyness is generally associated with gentleness, but there is nothing in shyness that makes one, more likely, a nice person.

Little shyness is understandable, but too much of shyness is a kind of social anxiety disorder.

Shyness has no logic. We may feel shy in the presence of an authoritative figure. We may feel shy when we are in unstructured and unfamiliar settings. Shy people look for closer bonds with people who are close to them.

One may feel shy in intimate encounters.

Shyness is subjective. In some, it is a social phobia. Social phobia may lead to loneliness.

Excessive self-focus and our preoccupation with our thoughts can lead to shyness.

Confident people are, perhaps, less shy.

There are behavioural and cognitive interventions to overcome shyness. Shyness interventions, perhaps, work better in group settings when they are with other people experiencing similar problems.

If one is comfortable with what one is, there is less possibility of self-doubt, there is less fear from failure, and there is less possibility of shyness.

Too much 'comfortable' with oneself makes one a narcissist.

It is said, "Shyness has a strange element of narcissism, a belief that how we look, how we perform, is truly important to other people."

A TOUCHING MIND

Touch is one of the finest expressions of being human.

A supportive touch can make all the difference. A sympathetic touch soothes depression and strengthens bonds.

Touch can lessen pain. It is a powerful medium of social exchange, fostering attachment, trust, and alliance.

Sometimes, a touch can be worth a thousand words.

Different kinds of touch express different emotions.

Fear, for instance, can be conveyed by a firm, motionless hold.

Sympathy, on the other hand, often reveals itself through holding, patting, or gently rubbing.

Most touches last no more than five seconds.

Yet, in these fleeting moments, we are capable of communicating distinct emotions—

just as we do with facial expressions.

Touch, it turns out, is a sophisticated signalling system
we are only beginning to understand.

When someone touches us, we first perceive its
physical properties—its speed, gentleness, or the
roughness of the skin.

Only afterward, depending on who touched us, do we
interpret its emotional value.

Neuroscience affirms this connection.

Touch and emotion converge in the brain's primary
somatosensory cortex, which encodes the texture of the
world: how smooth or rough something feels.

As sound is carried by the frequency of vibrations on
the eardrum, touch too, relies on timing and vibration.

When our hands move across a surface, the subtle
pulses of sensation help us read the world in silent
language.

Too often, we underestimate the power of a touch.

We must remember—we are not machines.

We cannot afford to lose faith in the human touch.

Touch a lonely heart with a tender hand,

and you will understand the quiet magic it carries.

ROBIN HOOD MIND

Robin Hood robbed the rich to feed the poor.

Robin Hood's mind roots for the poor, the weak, and the needy.

We all have some amount of Robin Hood mind. We all have some amount of fairness instinct. We get angry when we experience disparity, when we see injustice being meted out to the deserving.

It is fair to express anger if the reasons for anger are justified.

Often, people are angrier than the situation demands. That is not fair.

Like everything else, reciprocity requires fair play. A fair Robin Hood is respected, and his generosity becomes his asset.

We are generally not happy with what we have. We are more concerned about what others have. In the Darwinian language, it is not 'fitness', but 'relative fitness' that matters.

Maximisation of one's fitness is not enough to optimise relative fitness. Monitoring others' fitness and success is equally important. Relative fitness is related to 'relative deprivation'. Relative fitness doesn't get imbalanced if relative deprivation is under control.

The Robin Hood mentality is a kind of altruism: You scratch my back, I scratch yours. Robin Hoods expect reciprocation from the beneficiaries. They prefer generous reciprocators. The Robin Hoods don't like those favour-seekers who fail to reciprocate their favours in some form. Their conviction prompts them to choose favour-seekers.

Sympathy and gratitude (to those who helped the favour-giver in the past) play a big role in deciding the beneficiary.

Since natural selection prefers the strategy of 'keeping everything to yourself', can one have the evolution of fairness in the Darwinian world?

In the Darwinian world, there is space for other norms. We do many things that benefit others more than it does to us.

Robin Hood mentality is a kind of moralisation, and as Steve Pinker says, "Moralisation is a psychological state that can be turned on and off like a switch, and when it is on, a distinctive mindset commandeers our thinking."

MIND THAT DOESN'T NOTICE

Just ignore him.

Indifference is the most humiliating experience.

You say something — no one hears.

You ask — no one answers.

This is a form of invisibility.

Ralph Ellison wrote: "I am a man of substance, of flesh and bone, fibre and liquid — and I might even be said to possess a mind. I am invisible, understand, simply because people refuse to see me."

Invisibility is not absence, but denial — a refusal to acknowledge presence, voice, value.

José Saramago's novel Blindness imagines a modern city struck by a strange epidemic. One by one, people go blind. It begins with a man losing his sight at a traffic light. Soon, blindness spreads like a contagion. The government responds with fear — all the blind are confined in a former mental asylum. Chaos ensues. The only person who retains sight is the ophthalmologist's wife. She alone sees what others have become — blind not only in the eyes, but in the mind and heart.

Eventually, vision returns as suddenly as it vanished. People shout, "I can see! I can see!" But Saramago leaves us with a haunting question: Why did they go blind in the first place?

Did they ever really see?

He writes: "I don't think we go blind. I think we are blind. Blind, but seeing. Blind people who can see, but do not see."

Saramago points to a deeper vulnerability — collective blindness — when a society refuses to see itself, its injustices, its truths, its people.

When we stop seeing each other as humans, how can we possibly understand one another's pain, longing, joy?

Fritjof Capra recounts a therapy session.

A man shares his struggles — work, family, life's burdens.

The therapist listens. No judgment, no interruption, only presence.

At the end, the man breaks down and says,

"For the first time, I have felt like a human being."

Capra calls this an authentic meeting — two human beings in resonance.

The therapist helped lift the man's cloak of invisibility, not with insight, but with honest hearing.

Sometimes, paradoxically, blindness helps us see.

Jacques Lusseyran, who lost his sight at the age of seven, wrote: "I stopped caring whether people were dark or fair, with blue eyes or green. I felt that sighted people spent too much time observing these empty things."

Why do we fail to notice what is right in front of us?

Psychological studies reveal a startling fact: we overlook much of the world because our attention is narrow, selective.

We prioritize, we filter, we ignore.

We don't like distractions. We miss what we're not looking for.

Our minds are, in truth, selectively selective.

To see truly, perhaps, is not merely to use our eyes, but to remove the mental cloaks we wrap around others.

To unlearn indifference.

To learn presence.

To recognize that invisibility is not the absence of being, But the absence of being seen.

A LIAR'S MIND

We are habitual liars, and we play a liar's game at our convenience. Lying is often stressful, and defending a lie is not easy. We lie even when there is no apparent gain. We lie, out of respect for others. It seems, all fantasists find the experience of lying very rewarding. They find it very exciting that they can impress people by telling lies. We lie to reinvent ourselves. Perhaps our 'chronic feeling of emptiness' drives us to lying. Lying allows us to become what we are not.

In the Mahabharata, an elephant named Ashwatthama was killed. The rumour was spread that Drona's son (also named Ashwatthama) was dead. Drona wanted to check the veracity of the rumour from Yudhisthir. Yudhisthir said Ashwatthama (he said 'elephant' under his breath) was indeed dead. After hearing this, Drona laid down his arms. Draupadi's brother, who was waiting for an opportunity to kill Drona, cut off his head.

Yudhisthir lied, and also did not.

Not everyone can become a good liar. Professional liar masters the art of 'telling lies, the whole lies, and nothing but lies' in a manner as if it is 'the truth, the whole truth, and nothing but the truth'.

In many situations, we take umbrage at untruth. There is always more than one way to give a 'truthful' description of a truth. One can describe a situation highlighting a particular aspect that suits one's own perspective. Without lying, one can send across a wrong picture.

If the intention is to deceive, despite a no-false statement, a statement can be made with 'plenty of economy with the truth'.

More often than not, it is difficult to know the complete truth. Accuracy and sincerity are two virtues of truth. Truth indeed requires accuracy, but the 'whole truth' is the sum of 'part truths'. Unless all parts of the truth are available, 'truth' can't be 'whole'. And as someone said, there are only two ways of telling the complete truth — anonymously and posthumously.

Truthfulness is largely a matter of deciding what is reasonable to withhold.

Should one always say what one truly believes? One sociologist's advice: One should say what needs to be said in a given situation.

Like all other valuable things, truth has a shelf life. The half-life of truth is very short.

A BELIEVER'S MIND

On the other hand, a believer's mind likes to believe that it can correctly read the intentions of others. Our 'believing brain' finds meaning and pattern even when there is none. Our brain tends to ignore information that contradicts our beliefs.

Belief looks for patterns, and these patterns shape our understanding. Even our beliefs dictate our seeing. If it is true that belief dictates our seeing, it is also true that seeing dictates our belief system.

Simple logic says that something has a better chance of survival if it is advantageous to us. One of its corollaries is that belief in something can sustain only if that thing has proven its worth. The belief system will fizzle out if it is not worth believing.

God, for example, would not have survived had he not proven his worth.

What could be the evolutionary advantages of believing in God?

We all have experienced the illusion of God. The illusion is that someone up there is constantly watching us, and is also concerned about our moral lives.

When we know someone is watching us, we tend to behave differently. The feeling of 'being observed' makes one stop cheating.

'Someone is watching you' is our basic nature. Even committed atheists possess this nature. Supernatural beliefs promote altruistic behaviour and adherence to social norms. Some even say, atheism is probably the unnatural way to be.

God may be an evolved projection of our understanding of what God should be. But it is also true that our belief in the supernatural is natural. Our belief in the supernatural shall continue to remain so as long as the supernatural is useful to us.

Even the bread-giver has to earn his bread.

A GOSSIPER'S MIND

Gossip — we may not like it, we may denounce it, but we can't avoid it. It provides relief from monotony, a breather from routine. We can't be everywhere, but we want to know what's happening everywhere. Gossipers become our intermediaries — often unreliable, yet warmly welcomed. We rarely pause to ask how dependable they are. Instead, we accept what pleases the soul.

A gossiper doesn't hesitate to trespass into private territories. Their reputation thrives on their potential and factual access to the private lives of others. The more intimate the detail, the stronger their position in the social food chain.

We invest significant time and energy into gossip. On average, we spend 6 to 12 hours a day in conversation; gossip occupies anywhere between a fifth to two-thirds of that time.

It's a myth that women gossip more. What women may call 'kitty party chit-chat', men often label as 'networking' or 'exchange of ideas'. The perception differs; the function remains similar.

Gossip serves various roles — from gathering and disseminating information to providing entertainment and recreation. It is less likely to occur between strangers or casual acquaintances. Shared meanings, common histories, and social codes are essential. Gossip is an insider's privilege.

More than idle talk, gossip helps integrate complex social relationships. Through it, we gauge behaviours, align responses, and navigate social terrain. Without gossip, there would be silence, ignorance — even chaos.

A POLYMATHIC MIND

We are different because we don't have similar capacities.

Rabindranath Tagore, a multifaceted visionary, was a novelist, poet, dramatist, and artist. In a creative span of sixty years, he wrote and composed music for over

2,500 songs and created more than 2,000 paintings and drawings.

Leonardo da Vinci, the man behind the Mona Lisa, was not only a painter, but also a student of anatomy, biology, mathematics, and engineering. He was admired equally for his artistic finesse and for his physical prowess—proud of bending iron bars as much as of painting timeless masterpieces.

Aristotle was a philosopher, ethicist, logician, politician, astronomer, biologist—almost everything under the sun. These beautiful minds were polymaths.

T. H. Huxley once described a polymath as "someone who knows something about everything and everything about something."

Socrates offered a paradox of humility: "The only thing I know is that I know nothing."

A balanced mind is disciplined, creative, ethical, and respectful. It is not blind to anomalies within the group. A balanced mind is both a mirror and a window; it reflects the self and reveals others.

Yet, even among balanced minds, sharp ideological differences may arise. When balance tilts, when ideologies clash and egos collide, animosity and acrimony take the front seat. And then, the mind no longer remains beautiful.

A TEARFUL MIND

Human history is made of blood, sweat, and tears.

Tears are not merely expressions of emotion—they soothe, relieve, and cleanse. They reduce stress and often signal vulnerability. Sometimes they are strategic, drawing attention in public, while at other times they trickle quietly down the cheeks in solitude. Shower weeping is intense, like a storm; stream weeping is gentle, like a quiet release.

Tears communicate submission, foster trust, and evoke sympathy. They bind us in moments of helplessness and loss. But we also cry from personal conflict, rejection, anger, inadequacy, joy, and even the powerful emotions stirred by music and films. Crying, in a sense, is like exhaling, sweating, urinating, or defecating—a release the body and mind both need.

Tears have both healthy and pathological implications. They can flush out stress hormones and remove toxic substances. A good cry often follows periods of stress and brings a sense of calm. Traumatic memories may dissolve in the saltwater of grief. Yet tears can also be hysterical—born of confusion, sleeplessness, or psychological excitation. Some believe crying serves no purpose beyond discharging mental overload, allowing cerebral excitation to "flow away."

Not all tears are created equal. Emotional tears differ biochemically from those shed while chopping onions. And 'crocodile tears'—insincere displays—lack the psychic depth of genuine sorrow. Researchers have found that crying often improves mood. But, as Charles Darwin observed, tears need context to carry meaning. Without a mental, social, or narrative frame, tears are just moisture.

Darwin listed three reasons for the secretion of tears: primarily to lubricate the eye, secondarily to keep the nostrils moist for smelling, and importantly, to wash out dust and foreign particles.

Tears are as old as we are. "We came out of the ocean more than 400 million years ago, but we never completely left the sea water behind. We still find it in our blood, sweat, and tears," wrote Fritjof Capra.

Tears do not begin in the eyes. They begin in the mind—in a stir of emotion, in a memory rekindled, in a truth too heavy to hold. What the heart feels, the mind interprets, and the eyes release. A tear is thought made liquid, an emotion made visible.

Some tears come like storms, others like quiet rivers. But each drop carries the imprint of the mind—its longing, its ache, its surrender. To cry is not just to feel, but to process, to release, to begin again.

In tears, the mind confesses what words cannot.

OBESE MIND

We know that we should eat less and exercise more. Then why don't we follow what we know?

The fault lies in our heads. The urge to eat too much is wired into our heads. A multitude of systems in the brain encourage eating. Targeting one neuronal system is therefore not enough.

Our brains seem hungrier than our stomachs. We simply enjoy eating more. This habit of overeating evolved in us because we were not sure of the next meal. Our brain's prime directive thus has been to equip the body to meet this challenge. A consequence of this is that we developed obese prone 'default eat' system. We now need remedial measures to counter the effects of the system.

Overeating is compared with a phenomenon seen in drug addicts, who require greater amounts of their drug to feel the same reward. Chronic dieters are more susceptible than average to overeating.

Eating behaviours are also linked to areas of the brain associated with self-control and visual attention. Studies showed that successful weight losers had greater activation in those regions, compared with normal-weight and obese people, when viewing images of food.

When under stress, people like to eat high-calorie food. This is due to the association of stress pathways in the limbic system to the areas of the brain associated with seeking rewards. Eating high-calorie food is a reward-seeking behaviour.

Taming obesity probably lies in taming a hungry brain. Resetting the brain temporarily seems possible, but the problem is that the reset brain wants to come back to the original setting.

Another issue is the development of effective obesity therapy. This may require a combination of drugs that work simultaneously on multiple triggers of eating and metabolism. The therapy may also include, besides drugs, psychological or psychiatric approaches as well as exercises.

How cooking shaped the brain and society

The brain is a hungry organ. Though it constitutes only 2% of our body mass, it consumes nearly 25% of the body's energy.

The brain of Homo erectus was about 50% larger than that of its predecessor, Homo habilis. During this period, a significant reduction occurred in the size of their teeth. As more energy was rerouted to support brain development, other biological systems—teeth, jaw muscles, stomach, and intestines—declined in effectiveness. These organs grew less capable of processing a wide range of raw foods.

Yet, our ancestors adapted ingeniously to this evolutionary challenge. Despite a less efficient jaw and gut, they survived calorie shortages by developing smarter methods of food processing. They invented fire and mastered cooking.

Anthropologist Richard Wrangham observed, "The steady, accelerating pattern of brain growth was likely supported by shifts in diet as new food-procuring and preparation techniques steadily lifted the energy constraint on the brain's development."

Most animals do not have brains as large or as energy-demanding as ours. This is because they have not developed the means to meet the metabolic costs of a big brain. As our brains use energy, they also produce heat. Overheating could have become a fatal flaw—but the brain solved this with another innovation: sweating, a cooling system it controls.

The secret of our big brain, then, is cooking. Cooking is one of humanity's most significant innovations. It softens food, reduces fibrous content, and makes digestion far easier. One food scientist remarked, "Our dental anatomy is not designed for tearing raw meat from bone or chewing fibrous leaves for hours. It is designed for a diet that is soft, mushy, low in fibres, and easily chewable."

Without cooking, our ancestors would have spent most of their waking hours just chewing raw food to extract enough calories to survive.

Life becomes easier when we understand our biological constraints. Great apes have helped us grasp much about our own evolutionary path. It's estimated that around 250,000 to 300,000 years ago, cooking became widespread. And with it came a transformation in how we saw our world.

Cooking didn't just alter our diet—it reshaped our social lives. Once females began gathering and preparing cooked meals, they became vulnerable to stronger males who could simply take the food. Rather than gathering or cooking themselves, some males found it easier to steal. This introduced a new dynamic: the need for protection and negotiation. Perhaps this was the beginning of the complex human male-female relationship.

THE NEURAL DUET

No one truly loves to hate or hates to love. Yet love can turn into hate, and hate into love.

Both emotions can arise at first sight, but unlike their swift arrival, they do not fade with equal ease.

One can love a stranger—for in the unknown lies the thrill of mystery.

One can love someone deeply familiar, for in the known dwells the joy of recognition.

Love and hate can be both rational and irrational. The rational varieties are easier to understand and manage.

But irrational love or hate is often shaped by one's character. It seeks expression without necessarily seeking justification.

Such emotions look for occasions, not reasons.

Love and hate are more closely linked than we imagine. Neuroscience reveals that the brain's "hate circuit" shares pathways with the circuit of romantic love.

In romantic love, large areas related to judgment and reasoning are deactivated—perhaps explaining why lovers are often blind to flaws.

In contrast, hate suppresses only a small area of the cortex. Hatred sharpens focus; it seeks judgment, sometimes even vengeance.

Brain imaging studies show that the experience of social rejection activates the same regions as physical pain.

Emotional wounds are felt in the body, like a broken bone or a clenched gut.

And yet, a loving touch can transform everything.

It soothes the nervous system, lowers blood pressure, calms stress responses, and even dulls physical pain.

But this soothing effect appears only in genuinely affectionate relationships.

When our brain knows it is with someone trustworthy, it reallocates its resources.

Instead of bracing against threats, it begins to learn, to heal, to grow.

THE ART OF SELF-OVERHEARING

Our brain doesn't just think—it also monitors how we think. This act of mental eavesdropping helps us course-correct, keeping backup routes ready if our chosen path falters. But such vigilance can backfire. An insomniac, for example, lies awake checking if sleep has arrived—only to be kept awake by the very act of checking.

Viktor Frankl suggested a paradoxical remedy: don't try to sleep—try to stay awake. Let go of hyper-intention, and sleep may come uninvited. He also tells the story of a stammering boy who, while pretending to stammer to avoid a bus fine, found himself unable to stammer at all. Trying too hard to control an outcome can often reinforce the problem we wish to escape.

In moments of uncertainty, decisions must sometimes bypass reason. Self-overhearing involves pausing, listening inwardly, and sensing when to act from instinct. Rational people don't suppress emotion—they manage it. And at times, a touch of irrationality can be the most rational thing to do.

EMPATHETIC MIND

There are good and bad books, good and bad money, good and bad fats. Bad breath could be due to good food. At this moment, let us assume that good is desirable and bad is not.

Our specific question is: Is becoming good or bad in our control?

Some would say yes. But it is not such a simple matter.

Some regions of the brain act empathetically, often defeating the purpose of evil. Our empathy circuit determines our capacity to feel for others. Those who lack sympathy may have "a chip missing in their neural computer."

Empathy is more like a dimmer switch than an on-off button. A healthy empathy circuit enables us to feel others' pain and transcend a single-minded focus on our own concerns. If evil is the outcome of a malfunctioning empathy circuit, then becoming good, courageous, or heroic could also be a function of a well-developed one.

This suggests we are good or bad depending on the nature—and possibly the nurture—of our empathy circuit. In theory, one could become good or bad by manipulating this neural machinery.

But some neuroscientists argue that neural explanations alone are insufficient. Just because regions of the brain light up when we feel empathy doesn't mean they cause empathy; they may simply reflect it.

Empathy is more than a neural response—it is a skill: to understand another person's thoughts and feelings and to respond appropriately.

A DISFLUENT MIND

We are cognitive misers.

We prefer the surface to the depths, the familiar to the strange, the smooth to the jagged.

When things are easy to process—when names are simple, designs are clear, and words flow—we feel closer, safer, even more favourable toward them.

This is the psychology of fluency.

What is easy to process, we trust. What is familiar, we welcome.

Disfluency, on the other hand, feels distant.

When a name is hard to pronounce or a concept difficult to grasp, we feel more remote from it, and often more negative.

We think it's old if it's hard to remember.

We think it's far if it's hard to perceive.

Disfluency creates distance.

But this is not the whole story.

Though fluency is pleasing, disfluency has its place.

It is the invitation to think harder, to look deeper.

It compels us to engage with what we might otherwise ignore.

It slows us down—and in doing so, it opens a path to understanding.

Disfluency teaches us resilience.

It prepares us for ambiguity, for the uncertain future, for the messy realness of life.

Those early experiences of confusion and struggle?

These are not flaws in learning. They are learning.

Think of someone you believe you know well.

Now, try to recall ordinary facts about them.

You may be startled by your ignorance.

It's disfluency knocking.

An opportunity to know, not just to assume.

We are cognitive misers, yes.

But disfluency reminds us: meaning is not always at the surface.

Sometimes, it waits for those willing to search a little deeper.

MIND AND I

Mind, a product of habit, conditioning, environment, memory. has no mind of its own. It doesn't choose, it responds. It is a flowing stream, just the shape of what it holds.

Only the mind has mind. Mind is the sole seat of awareness. All meaning, identity, and choice emerge from mind. Mind is both observer and creator. It affirms consciousness as the core of existence. Without mind, there's no thought, no time, no I.

I exist because mind exists.

Mind generates thoughts like I am, I think, I feel. Identity arises from mental processes. Without the mind, there's no constructed "I".

 Mind exists because I exist.

The "I" is primary. It is the awareness behind changing thoughts. Vedanta posits the view that self (atman) is eternal, and the mind is its tool.

Mind is content; I am context.

We have emerged together,

To shape each other.

We are inseparable

In the art of becoming.

FUTURE OF THE MIND

Our neural suitcase is the most astonishing thing. The conventional view on brain functioning was that we are born with a set number of neurons, hardwired in a certain way. We lose connections and neurons as we age, and finally, the brain falls apart. Researchers now claim that neurons can change their connectivity, morphology, and strength of the connections in their early as well as later stages of life in response to new environments and experiences. New research has shown that the brain has a "use it or lose it" approach in neurological maintenance.

We suffer from future-obsession. We love to speculate what we will be like decades or centuries from now. We love the fantasy of encountering aliens far more intelligent than we are. The Fermi Paradox — seeming absence of intelligent alien life swarming around us, even though such life seems possible, hounds us regularly. For some, the intrusion of the digital age in a big way is a matter of great concern. Are we the 'soft and biological' humans? Or a more perfect 'hard, digital, and almost inconceivably powerful' is yet to evolve. "Extrapolating the trajectory of our current technological evolution suggests that with enough computational sophistication on hand, the capacity and capability of our biological minds and bodies could become less and less attractive," writes Caleb Schrf. A machine is error-free; natural evolution is error-prone. Is our blueprint, like many other blueprints, likely to be obliterated? Perhaps not. "Houdini believed that true telepathy was impossible. But science is proving Houdini wrong", writes Michio Kaku. Kaku says it is possible to read our brain by combining the latest scanning technology with pattern recognition software. Kaku envisages a mind that can videotape dreams. Our consciousness can be downloaded onto machines. There would be a possibility of transporting thoughts and emotions through the "internet of the brain". Kaku is optimistic about the future of the mind. "Perhaps one day the mind will not only be free of its material body, it will also be able to explore the universe as a being of pure energy. The idea that consciousness will one day be free to roam the stars is the ultimate dream. As incredible as it may sound, this is well within the laws of physics." Kaku says the mind is a hard engineering problem, and since fundamental laws of engineering are already known, it will be easier to understand and manipulate the 'computer of meat'. By mapping the "connectome", Kaku imagines, it should be possible to reverse-engineer every person's brain. Using the connectome, one can download oneself into a machine. When that is possible, your mind can live as long as that machine lives.

There is a worldwide interest in the reverse engineering of the brain. The major groups involved in the work have varied aims. The Human Brain Project aims to simulate the brain electronically on computers. The Brain Research through Advancing Innovative Neuro-technologies initiative aims to map the neurons of the brain directly. Another project aims to decipher the genes that control brain development. Reverse engineering the brain is bound to raise many questions, both technical and non-technical. Are we merely the sum of our brain's connections? In the absence of a good working model to understand consciousness, should we envisage the kind of future of mind that are being envisaged?

What significant things have happened in neuroscience in the past decade? Scientific American lists the ten most significant things that have happened in neurosciences:

(1) New sequencing technologies have boosted our understanding of the genetic pathways that spawn neurological and psychiatric disorders; quick identification of clusters of disease-related genes will likely transform the way we identify and treat brain disorders in the future.

(2) Mapping regions of gene activity to understand how the human brain works.

(3) The realization and exploitation of adult plasticity.

(4) The 'place cell neurons' that fire only when an animal is in one specific place but not in any other location.

(5) Memories are not like 'ink on paper' but more like 'inscribed in clay'; memory gets smudged every time you access it.

(6) Cognitive behaviour therapy that examines how one's thoughts and feelings influence behaviour and then introduces strategies to nix those maladaptive beliefs aimed at giving people hope.

(7) Switching individual neurons on or off with light, shining a light makes those neurons either more or less active and can elucidate their role in a behaviour or disease.

(8) Glial Cells play an important role in memory and learning.

(9) Neural implants for restoring lost brain function and intractable brain disorders.

(10) The brain has two distinct mechanisms for committing to a course of action: an automatic, unconscious way of thinking and a more deliberate and measured approach.

Understanding the human brain fully, perhaps, will never be possible. There will be ethical challenges. But there is hope. There is hope among neuroscience researchers that in another ten years' time they will find better treatments for conditions such as depression, schizophrenia, and Alzheimer's disease.

The list of yet unsolved problems in neuroscience is never ending. The problems include: what is the neural basis of subjective experience, cognition, wakefulness, alertness, arousal, and attention;

• How does the brain transfer sensory information into coherent, private percept, and the rules by which perception is organized?

• What are the features/objects that constitute our perceptual experience of internal and external events? How are the senses integrated?

• What is the relationship between subjective experience and the physical world? Where do our memories get stored, and how are they retrieved again? How can learning be improved?

• What is the difference between explicit and implicit memories? How plastic is the mature brain?

• How and where does the brain evaluate reward value and effort (cost) to modulate behaviour, and

• What are the limits of understanding thinking as a form of computing?

No one knows where our future lies. And yet, we will continue to make future projections.

MIND WEAVES VERSES

Mind weaves verses—

Words take flight,

Drifting, scattering, fleeting light.

Verses seem vague, often misunderstood—

Some rhyme, some float

In quiet hope of being withstood.

Open to interpolation,

Subject to extrapolation,

They echo in chambers of contemplation.

FLUID MIND

Moves like a river,

Shifting from place to place,

Adapting to contours of an ever-changing course.

Vulnerable, sensitive,

It thrives on swift connections—

Divergent thoughts,

Disparate situations.

Navigating inconsistent tides,

It maps the expanse of imaginary realms.

A NEURAL SUITCASE

Pack me carefully.

I am fragile; I fade with time.

Reshaped, mauled, even fabricated,

I'm a collage of the old and the new.

I commit subtle sins—

Just enough to distort,

Just enough to mislead.

WE BEGIN

We begin to breathe

before our lungs take shape.

We begin to digest

before our guts awaken.

We begin to think

before our thoughts are formed.

We are born, yet incomplete—

taking time to stand on our own.

We begin

only when we are ready to begin.

DARKNESS HOLDS LIGHT

Some have the gift of the mind.

For them, the loss of sight is not the end of sight.

Sightlessness is a paradox, a gift.

They see light rising, spreading, resting.

They turn sound into colour.

They are not afraid of wounds or falls—

But solitude dims their light.

For them, a closed eye is a world aglow.

MIND TOO HAS TWO HALVES

One bird dwell in the cage of comfort,

Content within its iron cell.

The other soars in freedom's skies,

Yearning for the boundless, wide.

Their worlds apart in vision's sway,

In conflict, their hearts may stray.

One sings for dreams and heights untold,

The other clings to the warmth of gold.

For in the flow of change and grace,

The true self finds its resting place.

Two birds

Mind too has two halves.

THE KNOWN

Knowing the known

is as demanding

as knowing the unknown—

perhaps even more so.

Just less lucrative.

MADE FOR EACH OTHER

Competition is made for cooperation,

The predator is made for the prey.

Contradiction exists for coalition,

Science is made for art.

Constructions are born for destruction,

Need is made for want.

Satisfaction exists to spark desire.

Optimism without pessimism is hollow.

Love and hate reside in the same space.

Free will is destined.

Theory without practice is ignorance.

Can you imagine zero without infinity?

Can you think of gods without demons?

Can there be reality without imagination?

Can you awaken without sleep?

Can freedom exist without responsibility?

Can it be called drawing if it's not worth tracing?

Isn't remembrance made for forgetfulness?

Without visibility, what is invisibility?

Without leaders, can there be followers?

Without teachers, students?

Can there be music without sound?

Complexity without simplicity?

Does one have a mind that is made for the other?

Perhaps one mind always waits

for the other to arrive.

A BEAUTIFUL MIND

A beautiful mind

strikes a delicate balance between

integration and differentiation,

convergence and divergence,

calm and restlessness,

competition and cooperation,

optimism and wishful thinking,

idealism and realism,

plasticity and rigidity,

tolerance and indifference,

faith and doubt,

acknowledgement and anonymity.

A beautiful mind

often, unpredictable,

misunderstood, disproportionate,

at times limited,

Yet, inspires mankind.

We all are born with a beautiful mind,

Some let it bloom; some leave it behind.

Some minds shine,

Some stay quiet.

AN ORDINARY MIND

Ordinary people have sound minds.

But in a world obsessed with being smart, can an ordinary mind be smart?

The ordinary mind is chaotic and fearful. It loves and hates.

It is intuitive and hungry. It is moral and vulnerable.

A loyalist and a whistleblower. It gossips, and it lies.

It is confabulated and fictional. Decisive and biased.

Lonely, yet crowded. Trapped, painful, violent.

Meaningful—and blind.

It makes deliberate mistakes.

It is curious, innovative.

It rebels at stagnation.

It craves variety, surprise, and the adventure of the unknown.

It daydreams.

It builds castles in the air.

The ordinary mind is big enough to wonder, small enough to change.

Yes, the ordinary mind can be smart,

*Because it knows that happiness is one of the cheapest
commodities it can buy.*

Ordinary people have sound minds.

*"A sound mind can neither be bought nor borrowed.
And if it were for sale, I doubt whether it would find a
buyer. And yet unsound ones are being purchased every
day," thought Seneca.*

THE DAY BONDS FADE

You forget the days and years,

Faces once dear disappear.

Memories drift like autumn leaves,

Carried away by the restless breeze.